GEOGRAPHICAL ECONOMICS

Is the unrestricted operation of the market economy compatible with the best interests of all society? If not, what are the economic and political implications?

With these basic questions in mind, Professor O'Sullivan provides a lucid introduction to geographical economics. Devoting separate chapters to the theory of location, agglomeration economics, travel, trade and transport facilities, he builds up an equilibrium model of the geographical economy, taking into account spatial and temporal variables and the uncertainties of cost, supply, demand and utility. He then examines the geographical aspects of economic growth in an analysis which provokes questions of equity and efficiency and their implications for regional policy.

Drawing on examples from Britain and the United States, the author points to the vital relevance of geographical economics in political decision-making.

Patrick O'Sullivan is Professor and Chairman of the Department of Geography at Florida State University.

GEOGRAPHICAL ECONOMICS

Patrick O'Sullivan

A HALSTED PRESS BOOK

John Wiley & Sons
New York

© Patrick O'Sullivan 1981

First published in paperback by Penguin Books Ltd 1981
and simultaneously in hardcover by
THE MACMILLAN PRESS LTD
London and Basingstoke
Companies and representatives
throughout the world

Published in the U.S.A. by
Halsted Press, a Division
of John Wiley & Sons, Inc.,
New York

Printed in Great Britain

ISBN 0-470-27122-1

Library of Congress Cataloging in Publication Data

O'Sullivan, Patrick Edmund.
   Geographical economics.

   (Geography and environmental studies)
   "A Halsted Press book."
   Includes index.
   1. Geography, Economic.   I. Title.
HF1025.086   330.9   80-39881
ISBN 0-470-2722-1

Contents

215740 1

Introduction

The Purpose of Geographical Economics

The things we worry most about are the ones which most affect our earnings and our living standards. A large part of the time we give to working things out and taking in information is given up to matters of income, the price of food, housing costs, fuel costs, taxation and government spending. Nor is this only true of the individual. Despite Plato's injunction that government should not be seen as home economics writ big, politics is largely a matter of housekeeping for the state. At either level human life is still dominated by having to ensure that material needs are satisfied. As individuals, family members and citizens we would like to be able to foresee events, whether we can control them or not. The power to predict improves the outcome in any area of life where control is possible. To buy goods, to order our finances and to invest in buildings, land and machines as best as we can to meet our needs, we have to guess at the shape of the future. Beyond wild surmise, such forecasting requires an understanding of how the world works. The explanation of events lies in the circumstances which conspire to give rise to them. Circumstance is a matter of place as well as time, geography as well as history. For many choices we make it is important that the place be right as well as the timing. The focus of this book is on the geographical circumstances governing the economizing of limited resources. The questions it raises will essentially be about the best places to produce, consume and invest.

The central issue in theorizing about the economy is the compatibility of the best interests of all society with the unfettered operation of markets in assigning resources to uses. Is it necessarily the case that the sum of individual efforts to achieve their own best ends, competing with each other via impartial market pricing, will give rise to a disposition of resources and bill of goods which is best for society as a whole? The way to answer this is by measuring the social worth of the array of prices and quantities associated with the balance of competitive markets, to see whether or not it is the most that could be achieved. The analysis consists of seeking discrepancies between the descriptive equilibrium of a simplified representation of the economy on the one hand, and a prescriptive optimum defined in terms of a social welfare objective for the same model on the other.

This exercise has largely been done in terms of a static equilibrium where the economy is conceived of as timeless, and its adjustment process instantaneous. A concession to time is sometimes introduced in categorical fashion by specifying immediate, short- and long-run adjustments. Expansion or contraction of production takes place in the short term but investment in new productive capacity only takes place in the long run. The processes of adjustment are deemed to occur instantaneously or in a discrete step between two categories of time. This is a contrivance for mathematical convenience and ease of explanation. The economy can, however, be conceived of as operating in continuous rather than epochal time, with processes of change having a temporal dimension. The balance towards which the economy is then construed to tend is a steady-state path, like the desired track of a remotely controlled rocket.

Whether the economy is conceived of as a static or dynamic entity, the main objective of theorizing remains the same. We desire to know if the equilibrium towards which the economy tends when not constrained by government intervention is efficient in terms of maximizing the well-being of the body politic. If not, the obvious next question is what intervention does best move the economy towards the collectively best configuration or growth path, and do the current interventions by government do so or not?

At the outset the nature of the economic problem needs the clarification provided by a definition of social welfare and discussion of its measurement. Chapter 1 introduces the quantity most relevant to questions of place and discusses its geographical dimension.

In order to address policy questions and employ measures of welfare with hope of coming to a sensible conclusion, we need to build up a comprehensive understanding of how the economy functions. For our present purposes in particular, we need to develop a sense of its geographical characteristics and workings. To this end one traditional mode of organization is quite valuable for constructing a picture of the space economy. We start with a series of partial equilibrium formulations representing how some elements of the ensemble work when all else is held constant or assumed away. This *ceteris paribus* approach allows for the isolation and close examination of the behaviour of selected parts of the economy. When the segment of the economy selected is conceived of as consisting of numbers of individual economic actors buying and selling goods and resources in markets, the designation 'microeconomics' applies. From these partial equilibrium elements of microeconomic theory, we can build up our mind's picture towards a statement of the requirements for a general equilibrium structure for the economy's geography. In this, all of the relevant quantities are allowed to interact simultaneously to achieve a state of rest.

The use of a detailed, microscopic specification of the quantities and prices of the economy's operation becomes too cumbersome and analytically intractable for seeking answers to policy questions. This is especially so when change processes and growth are addressed. In such circumstances recourse is had to lumping the quantities of the system into homogeneous aggregates such as consumption, capital and government expenditure. If the relations between these can be discerned and articulated in terms of some politically controllable variables, then interventions to achieve given social goals may be prescribed. Some degree of aggregation is necessary if we are to discover empirical, quantified relations for the prediction of economic quantities for policy purposes. This is occasioned by our limited capacity to measure and manipulate observations of the world.

The most crucial policy issues arise from changes in circumstances. We will not get far in a discussion of policy without contemplating its dynamics, the processes of adjustment of the economy. In order to make these manageable for analysis and measurement, various degrees and kinds of aggregation are appropriate, according to the level of resolution of the policy and processes involved.

When we seek a logical structure to grasp the essence of a process as extensive, massive and bewildering as is economic growth, then only the most simplified and aggregate model of the economy is tractable. Tractability in this context implies the ability to determine the conditions under which a steady-state path of growth may exist and remain stable, and its character in terms of the relations between descriptors of the economy.

Having constructed logical and consistent, albeit simplified, explanations of how the geography of the economy works at microscopic and macroscopic resolutions, considering both its timeless tendencies and the steps and tracks of change in its shape, we have the minimum requirements for an intelligent approach to political questions of the geography of resource allocation.

This book is organized to follow the above train of development. In Chapter 1 the aim of economic theorizing in providing prescriptions for political choice and action is examined in the geographical context with a treatment of welfare economics. Welfare criteria and measurements are introduced and their place in theorizing about locational behaviour and the practical evaluation of policies and investments is elaborated.

Armed with a notion of the purpose of theory and the quantities employed in its construction we can take our first look at a partial geographical theory in examining some explanations for the uses to which land is put and where people choose to produce and live. The spatial variable which is assumed given for this analysis is the cost of transport. Given the structure of transport costs, the exercise in Chapter 2 is to find the best locations for activities.

The introduction of geographical coordinates for transactions presents an element of differentiation which economic theory has found difficult to manage. Specifying the location of buyers and sellers injects an element of natural monopoly into market structure. Some locations are patently more advantageous in transport cost terms than others. The implications of this phenomenon for the outcome of the competitive process is discussed in Chapter 3.

Recognition of the spatial extent of the economy calls for some attention to potential variations in the enjoyment of what have been called agglomeration economies. These largely arise from the proximate location of many producers, workers and consumers. Attention is paid to this in Chapter 4.

The second type of partial geographical theories about the arrangement of the economy is concerned with the movement of goods and people. Given the location of production and consumption and the costs of transport, what is the best pattern of travel and trade? These constituents of the demand for transport are the subject matter of Chapter 5.

The remaining element of the space economy to be released from assumed constancy is the structure of transport costs. This is determined by technology, the geography of the transport network, the competing uses of this network and their locational requirements. Transport networks are in many instances publicly provided or, if not, they are extensive structures requiring some efforts at foresight for their construction. This component of the geography of the economy can be considered to emerge by deliberate design rather than as an accumulation of small market responses. The analytic framework with which we approach this matter, is then one of optimization. We presume that its designers sought the best arrangement of investments given some predetermined goal. This seems more appropriate than a description of competitive buying and selling by many participants finding a state of rest. However, at least the use by carriers and cars of the road network can be described as such a competitive process. It does, nevertheless, present a departure from the usual conditions assumed to prevail in a market. The congestion phenomenon gives rise to what can be a serious gap between individuals' perceptions of the cost of travel and the social cost of resources tied up in travel. Chapter 6, then, concludes an examination of network geography with the question of congestion and investment decisions.

The partial equilibrium models of locations, flows and networks presented in Chapters 2, 5, and 6 are all predicated on an assumption of certain knowledge of the present state of the world and perfect foresight. The discussion of geographical competition in Chapter 3 will first introduce doubt about the outcomes of actions into the analysis of locational behaviour. In Chapter 7 this question of uncertainty and its implications is treated more extensively. This is a most critical consideration in the context of investment decision-making, which is brought to the fore in the examination of transport networks in Chapter 6. The discussion of uncertainty will then largely centre on this need for prediction in choosing new productive capacity.

Having pieced together a series of representations in geographical terms of the relationships and behaviour that govern parts of the economy, the next step is to represent the workings of the whole. We need to see what can be done to articulate an understanding of the overall balance which the economy might achieve when all the interactions and relations work themselves out simultaneously. After formulating such a general economic equilibrium without reference to space, Chapter 8 examines the means and prospects of incorporating the places of production and consumption and transport of goods in such an analytic framework.

Change processes of the economy are considered in the three categories of time distinguished earlier. To start Chapter 9, we examine the immediate time span, in which prices and trading relations do not change, with Keynesian multiplier and input-output models of regional economies. The short-run adjustment of prices of traded goods and magnitude of trading relations between regions is addressed next. The theory of interregional trade, first introduced in Chapter 5, is translated into a form in which equilibrium prices and quantities can be calculated for a large number of regions. The mathematical programming format employed yields a revealing relationship between the price of the factor location, that is rent, and transport costs. This relation is perhaps the linchpin of location theory. Finally, the long-run adjustment process is explored in terms of the migration of people between parts of the world, the mobility of capital and the geographical spread of technical change and new products.

The investigation of processes of change in Chapter 9 provides a substantial prelude to the analysis of economic growth and its manifestation in the geography of the economy. In Chapter 10, the balance between population and capital necessary for sustained growth to occur is scrutinized. The inequities in economic conditions between parts of a single nation, never mind between nations, which confront us, lead this inquiry into questions of equity and efficiency and their implications for regional policy.

Our final chapter picks up the policy theme which runs through the entire work, amplifying the accounts with a discussion of mostly U.K. and U.S.A. realities. General and specific issues are raised to seek the right course for the good of all. The particulars of how the government ought to intervene in the operation of the pricing mechanism, and in regulating and providing facilities and services, are taken up. Even if the right answers do not emerge obviously, at least what we offer here may deepen understanding of the dilemmas involved in politically economizing the geography of our resources.

1. Welfare Economics and Geography

Before embarking on the description of how the interactions of buyers and sellers in a market balance out to a stable set of prices and quantities associated with specific locations, we need to give the exercise purpose. It was intimated in the introduction that the steady state, resulting from buying and selling untrammelled by government intervention, may not always be socially desirable. In other instances it may prove, on the contrary, to be in society's best interests. Under certain conditions the market may produce the best allocation of resources from the standpoint of society as a whole. It may, however, break down as a mechanism for achieving collective well-being. Such failures are the economically valid occasion for political intervention. The analysis of the potential gaps between market equilibria and social optima is the concern of welfare economics. Theoretically, this is a matter of trying to draw up consistent rules for deciding whether, by means of policy instruments, a change from one state to the other should be made. In practice this translates into identifying and measuring the material well-being and costs associated with the policy or investment options facing the public sector.

From writings on theory we can glean two reasonable rules to keep in mind when contemplating such issues. The sufficient conditions for a change in the economy to be socially desirable are: (i) that it results in a progressive redistribution of wealth towards the worse-off from the better-off and (ii) that those who stand to lose from the change cannot hope to profit from bribing the expected gainers to oppose the change. Underlying these criteria are two value judgements. The first is that an individual is better off if that person gets a selection of goods which stands higher in their ranking of choice. The second is that society's well-being is improved if one individual becomes better off and no one is worse off as a result.

Geography and Welfare

All policy decisions have spatial ramifications, insofar as social segregation and geographical specialization in occupation lead to income source and level homogeneity in particular places but heterogeneity in these characteristics between places. Indeed, territory is often used as proxy for income or industrial structure in attempting to achieve a more equitable distribution among persons, using policy instruments which control the allocation of resources between different regions of a country. This is perhaps more strongly a reflection of the territorial organization of political responsibility in representative systems of government.

Many public investments in capital works such as roads and dams, and public regulations, such as pollution controls, have their impact confined to certain localities. For such discrete changes of circumstance at local level, the usual procedure for evaluating the implications for welfare is to measure the change in utility involved. A measure frequently advocated and employed has been called 'consumer surplus'.

Consumer surplus is the sum of the differences between what people are willing to pay in the last resort for a particular good and whatever the actual price paid is. In the economist's fundamental diagram, this quantity is given by the area under the demand curve above the price line. This magnitude plays a central role in constructing a theory about the way the economy works geographically, being the quantity which the social system should operate to maximize.

In everyday administrative procedures for appraising the worthiness of particular public works and policies which have geographically differentiated impacts, this is taken as the appropriate measure of benefit. Thus it seems suitable that our discussion of welfare economics should largely dwell on the meaning and value of consumer surplus. While its application becomes more deeply ingrained in political and administrative institutions, the century-old controversy over its validity continues to flare from time to time.

Consumer Surplus and Utility

The notion of the differences between people's reserve price and the market price as a measure of the social worth of discrete changes in economic circumstances stems from the appraisal of transport investments and policies. Indeed, the idea first saw the light of day in the context of bridge construction in nineteenth-century France. To make the meaning and application of the measure clear, consider what is the correct toll to charge for the use of a bridge. In general either of two prices will raise the same amount of revenue, for example to recover the cost of a bridge. If, as in figure 1.1, demand slopes down to the right, total revenue increases as the price rises initially, reaches a maximum and then decreases. Thus, below the maximum there will be two prices associated with every revenue level. In choosing between any two prices c_1 or c_2 to raise a given revenue in a socially desirable fashion, the lower price, c_2, will clearly be preferable because it maximizes the net utility to users, or their consumer surplus. The consumer surplus associated with c_2 is $A+B+C$, which is larger than the volume A under a demand curve above c_1. In choosing between investment or policy options with respect to a particular good or facility, the difference between the consumer surplus accruing when nothing is done and after the change is instituted has been taken to constitute a measure of the benefit of the change.

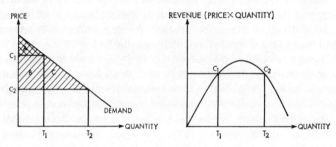

Figure 1.1

The use of the area under the demand curve as a measure of welfare must be qualified by pointing out that it works if a pound is a pound is a pound, i.e. if money has constant marginal utility. It implies that an extra pound when you have £10 is the same as an extra pound when you have £10,000. In addition, the completeness of the measure does depend crucially on whether the consumer spends more or less than before on the item in question after its price changes. If the price of a service falls due to an investment and the consumer thereby spends less on the service, he has increased disposable income to apply to other goods. He will gain additional surplus from the purchase of these. If he does not increase his consumption of the improved service at all, he will have the cost saving to spend on other things. If his demand is very elastic so that he increases his total expenditures on the service in question as its price falls, he will have to reduce his expenditure on other things and lose the surpluses involved. It can be argued that for the most part such effects are very small and, as long as the price change involved is not big enough to make additional income available for significant changes in purchases of other goods, consumer surplus is a reasonable measure of welfare. Theoretically correct measurements of welfare which circumvent this problem are unfortunately unworkable. 'Compensating variation' is the change in income which would be necessary to make the consumer indifferent to the change under scrutiny. 'Equivalent variation' is the amount of money which would leave the consumer at the same level of satisfaction as before the price change. The first measure is appropriate to answering compensation questions, whereas the second is the consistent index of welfare changes in all circumstances. It is held by some that the observable consumer's surplus will not necessarily move in the same direction as these theoretically satisfactory values for indicating utility changes, when measuring the welfare associated with alternative courses of action.

A rigorous condemnation of the general use of this measure arises from showing that the most stringent conditions have to be met in order for the marginal utility of income to be constant and for the area under a demand curve to measure welfare. Income increases due to a decrease in the price of one good must either be absorbed wholly by the good in question, and all cross elasticities of demand must be zero, *or* all income elasticities must be unitary. An approximation to these conditions will not satisfy purists.

From a more relaxed viewpoint, taking 'compensating' and 'equivalent' variation as the theoretically correct measures, it has been shown that the observable area under a demand curve gives a good approximation to these variations. Upper and lower bounds to the errors involved can be calculated with a knowledge of the consumer's base income and income elasticities of demand. In most circumstances it appears that the errors will be very small, overwhelmed by the errors involved in estimating the demand curve in the first place.

One matter which has not been fully explored is the relationship between individual and aggregate surplus. The theoretical formulations are usually phrased in terms of the individual. If we decide against the measure at the individual level, clearly it cannot be used at the aggregate level. If the measure is used we have to assume that consumers are similar, so that the aggregate can be treated as one individual. This additional assumption of homogeneity is obviously added cause for unease.

Controversy over consumer surplus is by no means at an end. However, enough has probably been said to underpin some practical judgements and propose some tests of suitability for use of the measure.

Geographical Theory and Consumer Surplus

The variable which lies at the heart of geographical economics is rent, the return which equilibrates the competition for the use of land. The value of this price is directly related to consumer surplus. In Chapter 2 we will see how classical location theory achieves an equilibrium such that land users are indifferent between locations. This condition of stability is arrived at when rent absorbs geographical variations in consumer surplus in the transport market. When this is so, rent added to transport cost comes to a constant value for all locations. From this it follows that changes in economic circumstances, such as cost-reducing investments in transport, can be evaluated in terms of their contribution to rent or equivalently to transport consumer surplus.

In Chapter 5 another classical underpinning of geographical economics, the theory of inter-regional trade, will be discussed. This, it turns out, can also be formulated in terms of maximizing consumer surplus as a measure of utility. The market equilibrium for trade in a good between two regions with fixed unit transport costs between them is found by maximizing the consumer surplus from the enjoyment of the good in the two markets, less the transport costs involved. When this formula is extended to the trade relations between many regions in Chapter 9, it reveals the reciprocal nature of rent maximization and transport cost minimization. Rent turns out to be equal to the amount saved on the transport of units of a good supplied by a particular location against units supplied by the marginal supplier whose rent is zero. Under assumptions of a common responsiveness to variations in transport costs and prices of goods, this rent is equivalent to consumer surplus obtained from the purchase of transport services. This is zero for the marginal purchaser of transport on the very edge of the market, and at a maximum for the most locationally advantaged participant in the market. Since each piece of land is unique in locational quality it is possible for its owners to discriminate perfectly between users in renting it out. The perfect discrimination of the land market is identical to that which would result from perfect competition. Under perfect discrimination, the incremental revenue from selling additional units of land is identical to the utility which purchasers place on the resource. Profit-maximizing by the owners of land results in prices which are efficient, because they mirror the incremental transport cost associated with a location. Prices are equal to marginal costs. The transport market consumer surplus which is maximized by this equilibrium is merely transferred to the owners of land. Whether this efficient solution is equitable is another matter.

Consumer Surplus in Practice

In choosing between investment or policy options with respect to a particular good or facility, the difference between the consumer surplus accruing when nothing has been done and after the change is instituted has been taken to constitute a measure of the benefit of the change. These were the circumstances which generated the notion in the first place. We will elaborate on this measure's use in transport decision-making in Chapters 5 and 6. As a measure of social worth it has become embedded in the evaluation of transport projects, where the public sector most frequently controls or subsidizes provision of the network. The measure is fused into the administrative procedures governing road and transport infrastructure investment in the U.K. and promoted as a benefit measure for transport development projects by the World Bank.

The economic questions which consumer surplus is employed to answer often have explicit geographical contexts. One source of market failure is the existence of natural monopoly in the form of a good or service whose costs continue to decrease as output expands over whatever is defined to be its market. Such industries as power, gas and water supply, telephone services and road, rail and waterway networks, sometimes identified as 'public utilities', are deemed to require government regulation or control to obviate the inefficiency of monopoly profits. These services are provided in comprehensive coverage of a spatially distributed market with fixed networks, making their supply natural monopolies, either locally or nationally, whoever owns them. Distance being perhaps the most potent differentiator of products, they are in a position to discriminate in the price charged for service according to where it is provided. The network structure of their capital is an enormous fixed element in costs which precludes easy entry and leads to diminishing marginal costs in most instances. Decisions on prices and investments in such industries usually have a geographical tag to them. Investment questions concern the structure and extent of the delivery network or the location and size of generating plants. Pricing policy is concerned not only with temporal discrimination, charging lower off-peak prices to deal with demand peaking and capacity problems, but also, at least for national monopolies, with geographical discrimination according to cost of delivery and elasticity of demand. Questions about the spatial pricing policy for phone calls are addressed by asking which policy maximizes observable consumer surplus.

The most significant practical investment applications of the surplus measure in cost-benefit analyses concern transport facilities. New or improved roads, railway-line extensions or closures, airports, bridges and tunnels have strongly localized effects. The assumptions about income elasticities and substitutes, upon which the measure stands or falls, are thus most frequently concerned with choices between locations for factories or homes in the long run and modes, frequencies and destinations of travel in the short run. The decisions and processes involved are the very stuff of geography. The advantage to society of constructing the motorways, the U.S. interstates or the various road and public transport systems planned for towns, depends on their impacts on travel patterns and land uses and whether these signify a net gain in well-being or merely a transfer of relative advantage from place to place and group to group. The nature of these impacts is still a matter for investigation, although heroic predictions have been made over the last twenty years on a very slender basis of facts. There is not yet clear evidence that increased accessibility, brought about by highway construction, for example, has a profound independent effect on the growth of economic activity in a locality. It has been conjectured that the building of the railway network in Great Britain had little impact on the geography of the economy, which was shaped by water transport, and a limited one on the growth of the economy as a whole. In the U.S.A., although it is clear that the construction of railroads resulted in large geographical transfers of activity, it is not clear that this had a major effect on national welfare. A case can be made that the same growth of wealth could have been achieved with a more compact economy geographically, using land more intensely, served by road and water carriers. This suggests that both the disposition of land uses and the transport costs, which would occur in the absence of the investment or policy decision in hand, are data which should enter the calculation of welfare improvements. Increases in demand for transport can arise from a more extensive use of land to produce the same output, the benefit accruing entirely to landowners or carriers of freight, if some degree of monopoly power exists in the transport sector.

If they are efficacious, the results of the transport improvements are to be seen in both travel behaviour and land use, one being a reflection of the other. In a caution against double counting by including travel and other market effects, it will be shown in Chapter 5 that the change in consumer surplus observed in the transport market merely summarizes the surplus changes in all markets for goods and factors whose prices are influenced by the transport improvement.

It is also necessary to point out that those who use the facility may not ultimately benefit from it. If the transport sector is monopolized it could reap the entire cost-saving as profit and pass nothing on, giving rise to no increase in demand or rent. There is a well-documented case which the World Bank investigated in Iran where this occurred. Merchants simply pocketed as profits the decrease in transport costs brought about by building a road, having a stranglehold on the transport of the products of the region through which the road passed. As we have seen in classic rent theory the benefit is entirely gathered as rent by owners of land. In reality much of the advantage may indeed pass on to those people other than the purchasers of transport. Among industrial users a firm with a heavy transport input may enjoy a cut in production costs. Depending on the responsiveness of demand for its products and the competition it faces, the firm may retain all of the saving as profit or pass it on to some of its customers in lower prices. Even if they do not travel on the new facility, property owners will garner the benefit of increased accessibility if it causes property values to rise. Transport benefits to renters may be reduced by the amount of any rent increase which property owners can impose to gain some of the benefit. The benefit to home owners will accrue partly in the form of increased property value. Over time the benefits fall to those in possession when the improvement is put in place, even if they sell. In the event of a sale the price will include the present value of the expected stream of transport benefits. In geographical terms it may not work to aim benefits at the inhabitants of certain localities in order to achieve income redistribution by the placing of a transport facility. It will not necessarily improve the lot of the occupants of the area, since the benefits may be passed on to owners of property, firms and consumers at large. The geography of these transfers provides vital information for making political decisions.

It is generally accepted that welfare judgements must take distribution into account as well as efficiency. There is in addition a political presumption in favour of equity between territorial constituencies. However, an equitable disbursement of funds in per capita terms between some regional units need not imply a similar disposition of benefits. The fact is that the benefits of transport or other public works spill over jurisdictional boundaries and the exclusion of non-residents from their enjoyment is impossible. For example, the improvement of rail commuting facilities within the city limits of Detroit will largely benefit suburban commuters, not those within the city's residential tax base, who are generally poorer. Even though the effects of losses and gains in local relative accessibility may cancel out, so as to signify little in terms of national increases in well-being, they can appear large changes to those immediately involved and can, thus, signify a great deal at least in local politics. Aggregate consumer surplus would provide inadequate evidence on which to judge the merits of projects in such circumstances. A map of the locations of gainers and losers is the minimal supplement required to judge the progression or regression brought about by the step under consideration.

Consumer surplus has been justified because it is available, as a measure of welfare, however imperfect it may be. It is certainly far more comprehensive than the commonly accepted National-Income measure of well-being which deals only in market prices. National Income represents only the first-order effect of a change in price, depending on the difference between price times quantity before and after the change. Consumer surplus at least incorporates the second-order effects, by taking into account the area under the demand curve between the price times quantity values before and after the change. It does, however, rest on the premise that the benefits to each member of society can be added up without regard to the individuals who enjoy them. There are circumstances where this is within the bounds of political prudence, indeed a politically desirable stance. Despite recent departures, it remains an underpinning of representative government that undue discrimination between citizens is undesirable.

A practical example of the application of this homogeneity assumption is the decision by the U.K. Minister of Transport, voiced in 1969, to employ a single value of time for the calculation of transport benefits, implying a constant and common marginal utility of time and income. For universally provided facilities, say, in funding local road improvements, where the investments are spread geographically more or less in accordance with the size of the population, and where the benefits are small and diffused to many people, an assumption of homogeneity with no regressive bias in the benefits seems reasonable. In deciding on the allocation of a fixed budget among a large number of similar uses, consumer surplus, which can be estimated from known present volumes and speeds and good guesses at future volumes and speeds, does seem likely to provide a consistent and unbiased ranking criterion.

For larger projects, arising more sporadically in time and space, whose effects are geographically confined, say, commuter rail or limited-access roads, where there are potentially stronger locational effects, then total consumer surplus may be inadequate as a welfare criterion. A new rail line or a motorway imposed on the fabric of a town or the Channel Tunnel spring to mind as awkward cases. Total surplus will fail to signal distributional outcomes, which may be of crucial significance politically. Wisdom in making judgements on whether the circumstances being addressed represent too violent a departure from the requirement that benefits have constant value, no matter who gets them, is at least partially a matter of geographical knowledge.

The theoretical employment of consumer surplus as a normative optimand to compare with competitive equilibrium is subject to the same strictures. If the real circumstances being addressed do not represent too violent a departure from assumed constancy of the value of money, then consumer surplus may be a satisfactory measure of social desirability.

In discussing welfare we have concentrated on one measure of social worth. This was done because it is used widely, both in practice and in constructing theory about the spatial structure of the economy. Our survey, in providing some clarification of the definition of a socially optimum arrangement and a market equilibrium, and offering a measure to apply to gauge disparities, has provided a theme and a purpose for our subsequent theoretical developments.

Readings

General treatments of welfare economics include: P. Bohm, *Social efficiency: a concise introduction to welfare economics*, Wiley, New York, 1973, and T. Scitovsky, *Welfare and competition*, Irwin, Homewood, Illinois, 1971.

A cautionary note is sounded in: J. M. D. Little, *A critique of welfare economics*, Clarendon Press, Oxford, 1950.

The application of welfare economics is considered in: E. J. Mishan, *Cost-benefit analysis: an informal introduction*, Allen and Unwin, London, 1971.

The seminal work on consumer surplus by J. Dupuit appeared in the *Annales des Ponts et Chaussées* in 1844. Translated as 'On the measurement of utility of public works' in K. J. Arrow and T. Scitovsky (eds), *Readings in welfare economics*, vol. 12, Irwin, Homewood, Illinois, 1969, pp. 255–83. The genesis of recent controversy over this measure is P. A. Samuelson, *Foundations of economic analysis*, Harvard University Press, Cambridge, Massachusetts, 1947, pp. 194–5. The current champion of the measure is: R. Willig, 'Consumer surplus without apology', *American Economic Review*, no. 66, 1976, pp. 589–97.

The use of the measure in analysing geographical policy questions is exemplified by: M. J. Beckmann, 'Spatial price policies revisited', *The Bell Journal of Economics*, no. 7, 1976, pp. 619–30.

The theoretical relationship of consumer surplus to geographical variations in prices and to location is expounded in: P. A. Samuelson, 'Spatial price equilibrium and linear programming', *American Economic Review*, no. 42, 1952, pp. 283–303, and B. Stevens, 'Linear programming and location rent', *Journal of Regional Science*, no. 3, 1961, pp. 15–26.

2. Land Uses and Locations

The Value of Land and Transport Costs

We have identified in partial manner a triad of elements of the space economy for investigation one at a time: land uses, flows and networks. An inquiry into their independent workings and intermeshing must start with an explanation of the use and value of land, given the costs of transport. For clarity and simplicity of exposition, the effect of the structure of the transport system on the arrangement of uses can be neutralized by invoking the myth of an isotropic plain with equally costly movement in all directions from any point. The results generated in this Euclidean space may then easily be mapped into the space of an abstract, symmetric transport network, and with a little more difficulty into the unique particulars of geographic space, as we shall see in Chapter 6.

To get the clearest view of the causes of land's value and uses, we can construct a simple geography which removes from our ken everything but what we believe at the outset to be the most potent explanatory variables. In this abstract setting it is possible to deduce an unambiguous response of producers and consumers to this simplified environment in terms of where they locate and what value they place on land. If the general tendencies deduced seem to accord with the real world, then the theory put forward can be counted a worthwhile conjecture about the processes involved.

Let us suppose that the isotropic plain is connected with the rest of the world by a railway line which has only one station at the central point of the plain. This singular focus becomes the place of buying and selling any marketable surplus produced by the farmers of the plain. Since our fictional economy already has many of the marks of the American High Plains, the Pampas, the Steppes and the Murray-Darling Basin, it seems appropriate to let the potential surplus be in just one crop, wheat. This is bought at the central point for a given world market price of £p per ton and any amount produced will be bought at this price. The demand for wheat is thus perfectly elastic, as shown in figure 2.5c. The evenly distributed farmers have a choice of subsistence, or subsistence plus commercial production of wheat. They will only indulge in commercial agriculture if it yields a surplus of income over outlay. The land is equally productive everywhere, yielding 1 ton of wheat per acre. (This is not unrealistic, having been achieved in England in the 1880s.) The crop is produced with fixed inputs of labour and capital per acre, costing £x per ton. The farmers will be induced to use some of their under-employed time and resources on the cash crop if the difference between production cost plus transport cost per ton and the fixed price at the centre is positive. If the transport cost is £b per ton per mile, then the margin of commercial cultivation will lie where the net price becomes zero, at a distance d_m in figure 2.1.

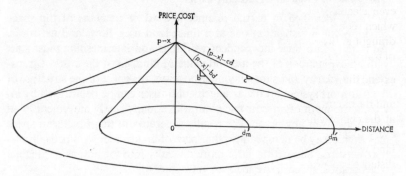

Figure 2.1

At that point: $(p-x)-bd = 0$. The area of commercial cultivation and, thus, total production, will be πd_m^2 acres or tons since yield is one ton per acre. It seems clear that the higher the price at the centre, p, the further out the margin of cultivation will be and the greater the quantity produced. Thus, the supply curve for wheat will slope up to the right as in figure 2.5c.

The surplus of market price above production and transport costs is greatest at the centre of the plain where transport cost is zero. For the marginal commercial wheat farmers, the cost of transporting the product has nearly eaten away the difference between price and production cost entirely. If there is an active market for land, then the advantage of greater accessibility represented by this surplus of income over outlay will induce a greater price for land at the centre. The per acre price of land will decrease from there to a minimum value where cash crop production ceases. The encouragement to compete for land and to change locations and land prices will only evaporate when a set of prices per acre has been arrived at which equalizes returns to all locations. That will occur when the values of land equal the values of the surplus plotted in figure 2.1. The value will be at a maximum of $p-x$ per acre at the centre and zero at the margin where net receipts are zero, i.e.

$$d_m = \frac{p-x}{b}.$$

The total amount of this surplus or rent would be the volume under the cone in the figure, i.e.

$$\frac{\pi d_m^2(p-x)}{3}.$$

The influence of transport cost structure on the value of land becomes even clearer if we can imagine the introduction of a technical advance which reduces cost per ton mile of transporting wheat. Suppose the use of draught animals instead of lugging bags on human backs reduces the cost of transporting a ton of wheat a mile from b to c. The effect of this will be to extend the margin of commercial cultivation, for if $c < b$ then $\frac{p-x}{c} > \frac{p-x}{b}$, and the circumference will shift to $d_m' > d_m$ in figure 2.1. The value of land at the centre will remain the same, for transport costs are zero there. At every location removed by some distance from the centre, the value of land will, however, increase. The value of the reduction in the friction of distance brought about by the innovation can be measured by the increase in rent which is the difference in volume between the two cones in the figure

$$\frac{\pi d_m'^2(p-x)}{3} - \frac{\pi d_m^2(p-x)}{3} \quad \text{i.e.} \quad \frac{\pi(p-x)(d_m'^2 - d_m^2)}{3}.$$

This would also be a measure of the increase in consumer surplus in the market for transport; an equivalence which we shall return to in Chapter 5.

An historical example of this effect can be seen in the shift of the Wheat Belt into the Great Plains after 1880, pushing out open-range grazing as railway construction reduced grain transport costs.

The value we have ascribed to land has been called economic rent, a return to a fixed factor earned because of the scarcity of some quality it possesses. In the case we have outlined all of this rent and its variation result from differences in accessibility. The prediction of a decrease of the price of land with distance from the market is borne out admirably by a map of U.S. agricultural land values (figure 2.2). The value of property per acre does indeed decline with distance from metropolitan markets. This is especially true of the Midwestern section where no enormous differences in soil, terrain and climate accompany the effects of accessibility. In reality soil characteristics and physique do modify the simple regularity with transport costs we have theorized here. Warm loams command higher

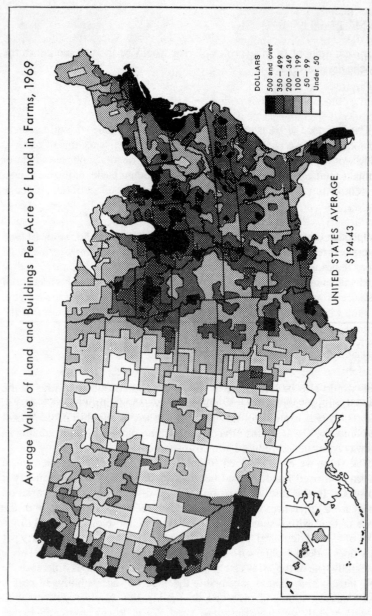

Average Value of Land and Buildings Per Acre of Land in Farms, 1969

DOLLARS

500 and over
350 — 499
200 — 349
100 — 199
50 — 99
Under 50

UNITED STATES AVERAGE
$ 194.43

Figure 2.2 Source: After U.S. Department of Commerce, Bureau of the Census, *1969 Census of Agriculture, Graphic Summary*, 1973, p. 20.

prices than acid sands or cold, damp clays. On the map the higher value of the Mississippi bottom lands' silt loams and loess between Cairo, Illinois and Vicksburg, Mississippi, stands out as markedly arising from the lie and quality of the land. For our purposes it is sufficient to note such possible modification to our simple scheme.

The trade and transport functions of the central town of the isotropic plain would employ labour in non-agricultural pursuits, and some of their food needs would generate a further demand for commercial agricultural production. For simplicity let their needs be represented by one product, say, milk, and suppose they can buy the other item of their diet, grain, at the going world price. The question which arises is: how will the production of this second agricultural product be accommodated, given the alternative use of land for the export production of wheat? Whether and where farmers produce milk or grain will depend on the ability of producers of the two products to pay for the use of land, or the rent they can pay. To deal with competition between two forms of production we have to have a more general expression for rent-paying ability than the one above. The ability to pay depends on potentially different yields per acre for different crops as well as different transport costs per ton mile, market prices and production costs. In this case rent must be written:

$$R_i = T_i(p_i - x_i) - T_i c_i d$$

where T = the yield in tons per acre and the parameters p, x and c are specific to crop i. The production of each crop will be governed by such a relationship and the crop whose value of R is greatest at any particular distance from the centre will prevail in competition for land at that location.

Let us suppose that dairy farming yields two tons of product per acre in a year, compared to one ton of wheat. Furthermore, because it must be delivered in small quantities every day, the total cost of transporting a ton of milk is much higher than that for less perishable wheat, which is shipped in large quantities once a year. We will presume that the input of labour and capital per acre is the same for both wheat and milk. Let the price per ton paid at the central town be higher for milk than for wheat. Under these circumstances the rent surfaces for milk and wheat might look like those in figure 2.3.

Given its higher transport cost per ton mile, the slope of the rent curve for milk is steeper than for wheat and, given its higher yield and price per ton, its rent at the market itself is greater than for wheat. Over the range OB, both dairying and wheat are feasible products; however, over the radius OE, dairying offers the superior rent and will thus oust wheat from the use of land. Wheat takes over at E where high transport costs have eroded the

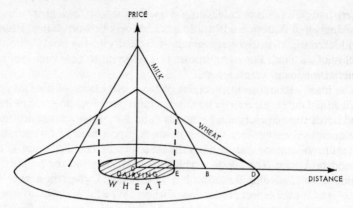

Figure 2.3

advantage of dairying in favour of wheat, which predominates out to the margin of commercial production at D. The equilibrium land uses are shown in figure 2.3 and the equilibrium rents are shown as the upper envelope surface in the figure, consisting of the dairying rent surface out to a radius of OE and of that for wheat for the segment from E to D.

In order for competition between products to yield such concentric rings of land use about the market, the rent curves for different forms of production obviously must cross at some juncture, as shown in figure 2.4a. The rent curve of one crop must have a steeper slope $(-T_1C_1 > -T_2C_2)$ at the same time that its intercept value on the central axis is greater $(T_1(p_1-x_1) > T_2(p_2-x_2))$. On the contrary, if a crop's rent function has a flatter slope $(-T_1C_1 < -T_2C_2)$ when its intercept is greater $(T_1(p_1-x_1) >$

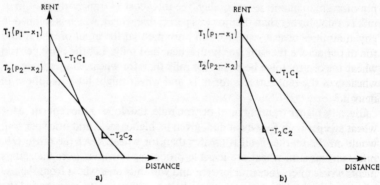

Figure 2.4

$T_2 c(p_2 - x_2))$ as in 2.4b, then no rings will form and one crop will predominate and the other will be excluded. This analysis can easily be extended to more than two products.

So far we have taken the price of milk to be a given and constant and determined quantity, produced as if demand for milk were perfectly elastic, i.e. as if any amount will be taken at the given price, the condition we prescribed for the demand for wheat. The demand for milk is, however, local and is likely to respond to its price. The higher the price of milk, the lower the quantity demanded. Let us suppose that milk production preceded the extension of commercial wheat acreage. The price of milk at the market would be determined where supply and demand are equal, at p_m^1 in figure 2.5a. This price gives rise to a rent surface M_1 in figure 2.5b. The

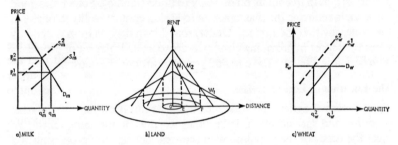

Figure 2.5

region is now opened to the world wheat market represented by the horizontal demand curve in 2.5c, generating a rent surface for wheat W_1 in 2.5b. This cuts back the supply of dairying land, and thus milk, to that produced by the area within radius OE of the centre. This reduces the supply of milk available at every price, back to S_m^2 in 2.5a. This causes the price of milk to rise to p_m^2, thus raising the rent that milk producers could pay at every distance from the centre to M_2 in 2.5b. This shifts the margin for dairying out to OF and the quantity to q_m^2. Since the demand for wheat is perfectly elastic at P_w, the adjustment process ceases here, with wheat being grown from F to D. If, however, we had assumed that the demand for wheat did vary with price, then the cutback in its supply because of the expansion of milk production would lead to an increase in wheat's price and thus the rent surface for wheat would be raised. This would cut into the dairying acreage, shifting its supply curve and raising its price and rent surface, and so on. At each round the size of these adjustments would become smaller, converging to stable prices, rents and shares of acreage between dairying and wheat.

Economic geography is replete with evidence of such annular land-use structure and debates over which product should be where in the order of the rings. In trying to nail such an explanatory construction onto the landscape there is a danger of falling prey to a strange Stoic and Hegelian misconception that the world is a distortion from some pristine, Euclidean reality of essences: that the heavenly blueprint is warped by man's stupidity along with the failure of the surface to achieve homogeneity. Indeed, the term 'distorted' is often used to describe a mapping from the theoretical space into real geography. We should keep in mind that it is theorizing which distorts reality into simplicity, as making a map warps and condenses a bit of the globe into two dimensions. What is important is the reality in its rich confusion of cause and motive and delightful diversity. Theory is a map to help us on our way to understanding. Sometimes good theories, in reducing the phenomenon to basics, contort reality strongly, in the same way that the London Underground map departs from geography more than most in providing clear answers to a particular set of problems. You certainly wouldn't use it to find your way around the houses.

The Location of Local Services

As commercial agriculture generates more wealth it nurtures the market economy and specialization. It becomes worthwhile for entrepreneurs to meet the needs of the populace with services such as food processing and sales of implements, household goods, fuel, clothes, even exotic foodstuffs. Many of these activities could not reach the entire local economy from one outlet. The question then is how would several outlets for one product dispose themselves locationally to best advantage. As the basic building block for the structure we may take the processing of the staple diet, milling wheat for household consumption, and assume that it is the service with the most limited market area within which an entrepreneur can make a living. The pattern of mills can be given one fixed point by presuming that a miller will certainly locate at the central town of the plain. Given the uniformity of population already implied, they will require a similar amount of flour per household per month. The choice must be made between taking the requisite amount of grain to the mill and paying for its grinding, or doing it themselves. They know the expenditure of labour and equipment involved in the latter and thus have a maximum payment for milling the fixed quantity, consisting of the charge for milling, the cost of transport to and fro and the cost of storage. They will pay any price up to that maximum for the fixed quantity, which is just less than the cost of doing it themselves. We can imagine that some trade-off is possible between storage and transport; people further from a mill may travel less frequently and store more. For simplicity let us consider these costs compounded in a transport cost which increases regularly with distance from the mill. The demand curve of a farmer for milling will look like figure 2.6a. Since farmers are at different distances from any potential mill location, then their maximum prices will vary with distance and the miller will be faced with a downward-sloping demand curve for this service, as in figure 2.6b.

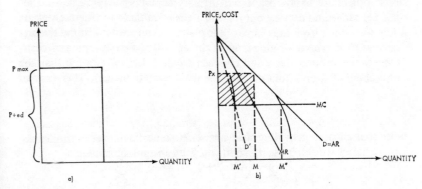

Figure 2.6

As he reduces his price the radius of his market area increases and thus the quantity demanded. At the market centre a high price will attract the few people whose transport costs are negligible. Since the miller must offer the service to everyone at the same price, as he wishes to extend his market area he must reduce the price by the amount of transport cost incurred at the maximum radius he wishes to capture.

In deciding how far to extend his market the miller's motive is profit maximization, i.e. maximizing the difference between total costs and total revenue. We can suppose that, beyond some minimum threshold level where commercial milling becomes viable, the cost of production per ton does not change significantly over the range of output in view. Thus the marginal cost curve for milling, MC, will be flat as in figure 2.6b. Since the demand curve the miller faces slopes down to the right, the average revenue achieved, as output expands, declines in unison with the demand curve. As the average revenue is declining, so the change in total revenue as quantity increases will be falling more rapidly. The extra revenue achieved by serving each additional customer, marginal revenue, MR, will decrease with quantity as shown in figure 2.6b. The miller will seek a level of production where the difference between total cost and total revenue is maximized. This will be achieved where the extra revenue from the last unit sold just equals the extra cost involved. In figure 2.6b this is where the marginal revenue curve and the marginal cost curve intersect. This quantity projects up onto the demand curve to give a price p_x and surplus profits equal to the shaded area.

The price p_x at the mill site will imply a maximum transport cost and thus, a market radius of, say, r miles. Seeing the profitability of this enterprise others are likely to ape our primary capitalist, leaping beyond his market range and carving out market areas of radius r for themselves. As they spread out from the centre of the plain, six can cluster around the first circular market area forming tangent circles with non-overlapping markets, then twelve around these and eighteen beyond. Let us suppose that the next chain of twenty-four exhaust the plain as in figure 2.7. This division

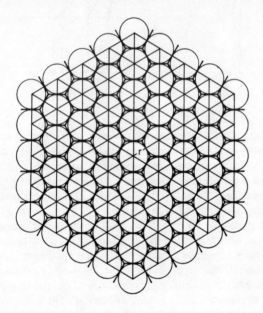

Figure 2.7

of the market gives rise to the hexagonal packing of market areas and a minimum of unserved interstices.

When the region has filled with these monopolized local market areas, there is still an incentive for entrepreneurs to seek entrance to the business. Large monopoly profits are being earned, and a share of them can be obtained if you can capture a bit of the market greater than the threshold below which costs become prohibitive for commercial production. The first of these new entrants is likely to go for a location alongside our first miller at the centre of the plain. Actual entry would cut back the demand curve of the existing miller by the amount the new entrant captured, each lowering his price to retain a market share. New competitors could potentially join the original miller at the centre until the share of the total demand which each competitor captures is just above the threshold production level, say at D' in figure 2.6b. At this point everyone would have to be charging a price equal to marginal cost. At any higher price, costs could not be covered by revenue. The original producer can preclude new entrants from capturing a share of his market, and live in hope of monopoly profits in the future, by reducing his price to the marginal cost equal to the average revenue level, achieving sales of M''. There is no attraction to competitors at all at this point. In lowering his price the defending miller extends his market area, encroaching on the unserved interstices and the market area of his neighbours. This encroachment will call forth a similar response by them to defend their markets. Faced by this threat of entry in their markets and encroachment on their periphery, they will be similarly obliged to reduce their prices to the level where average revenue equals marginal cost. In figure 2.8 as A reduces his mill price from 2 to 1, so the delivered price of the service will decrease from 2,2 to 1,1. This will shift the margins of equal delivered price from M to M'. In order to maintain the size of their markets, producers at B and C will be forced to reduce their prices to $1'$ from $2'$, pushing the market margin back to M. Such a price reduction will then obviously impart itself to the next layer of market areas around the core and so on to the edge of the plain. The outcome in most circumstances will

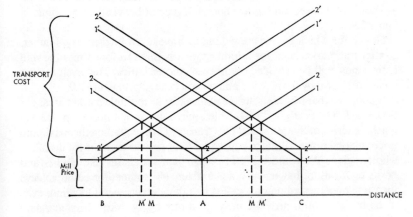

Figure 2.8

be an extension of service to all parts of the region at a uniform price equal to the marginal cost of production. The market boundaries will become straight if our farmers discriminate perfectly between suppliers in transport cost terms. The result will be an hexagonal market area structure as shown by the heavier lines in figure 2.7. The overlap of circular market areas and equal division of this overlap will result in the actual demand curve of each miller turning down beyond a radius *r*, as shown in figure 2.6b. The final quantity sold will be less than if the original lone miller sold his output at a marginal cost price. Actual entrance of new producers or a threat of entry and the interlocking of markets in terms of the delivered price of the service on offer will then give rise to a price to be expected from perfectly competitive circumstances, despite the fact that sellers face downward-sloping demand curves.

All other services whose delivered price contains the same maximum distance component, and which will thus have the same market range, *r*, will locate along with the mills. These might comprise food stores and public houses. The maximum market range of other goods, like farm tools and implements, might be larger. People make purchases less frequently and are willing to travel further to buy them. The market areas for these goods, generated by the process we have just described for milling, will be greater. Since there are economies to be derived from proximate location, from the enjoyment of collective goods, and by providing the customer with the opportunity to combine the purposes of a trip, our implement dealers will choose a selection of existing mill locations. If the market areas for implements are between one and three times mill market areas, implement sellers will locate at the central town and at the centres of a lattice of market areas as shown by the second lightest lines and second heaviest set of points in figure 2.9.

Goods for which people are willing to travel even further, say, lumber, so that the market area for a lumber yard is three to four times the mill hinterlands, will be provided on an even coarser lattice. The seven market areas are shown by the heaviest and biggest hexagons in figure 2.9.

It could be that this exhausts the plain as far as multiple market areas are concerned. The next good up the hierarchy may have a maximum market reach, in terms of marginal cost plus transport cost equalling the maximum price customers are willing to pay, equal to or greater than the radius of the whole region. We could think of once-a-year purchases like clothes and boots or furniture having such a character. No competitor could achieve the same uncontested market radius by taking a peripheral location, even if the initial, central provider prices at a monopoly price where marginal cost equals marginal revenue. However, actual competition at the centre,

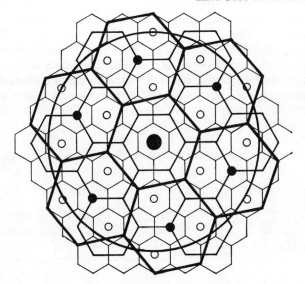

Figure 2.9

or fear of it, will force the price down to the level at which marginal cost equals average revenue, thereby serving the whole plain from the central city.

The result of this process is a hierarchy of central places. At the head of this hierarchy is the largest town at the centre of the plain, providing all services to an expanding series of market areas, until the highest-order good is provided to the whole local economy from the centre alone. At the next level there are towns which provide the most local good, plus some good of intermediate market reach, to a section of the regional economy. Finally, there is a fine mesh of places providing only the most local service. The hierarchy in our example has four levels with specialization in the two intermediate levels. There are 61 mill sites, 19 of which are selected as locations by implement dealers, while another 6, plus the central town, will be chosen as sites for lumber yards. The central point alone will house a clothes, boots and furniture store.

The hierarchical arrangement with hexagonal networks of market areas can obviously be generalized to treat a series of differing ranges and thresholds. The same structure can be applied to analysing the arrangement of shopping facilities within larger towns as well as in the country setting. The hierarchy rising up from corner shops to local parades, suburban shopping centres to the downtown congregation, is explicable in similar terms to the ranks of villages, towns, provincial capitals and the metropolis.

The hierarchical arrangement can be seen clearly where the physique of the land simplifies the arrangement of settlements. A long, narrow peninsula essentially collapses the structure of central places onto a line. The Corcaguiney of West Kerry in Ireland, extending westward into the Atlantic from the county town of Tralee (figure 2.10), suits admirably as such an example.

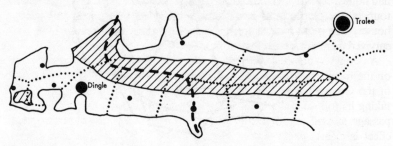

Figure 2.10

Tralee, with a population over 10,000, serves the entire county, including the peninsula, with local government, administrative and high-quality retail services, having department stores, women's fashion clothing stores, car and implement dealers, and a wide range of specialities such as jewellers. The county newspaper, the *Kerryman*, is published and distributed from Tralee. Dingle, with a population around 2,000, shares with Tralee in providing banking services, hardware, feedstuff, groceries, doctors, dentists, barbers and hairdressers, cinema and dance-halls, building supplies and lumber, principal post offices, secondary schools and a creamery for butter-making to the area. Tralee and Dingle about divide the peninsula in half in serving these functions. The hierarchy of administration and law, courts and guards' barracks follows the same lines, with Tralee containing the higher echelon. The church on which most hierarchical arrangements are modelled, however, chose Killarney to the south rather than Tralee as the seat of the Bishop of Kerry and cathedral site, with Tralee and Dingle sharing similar status.

The most local level of services, sub-post office, general convenience shop, bar, petrol pump, church and national school are provided by a scattering of places of ten houses or so, varying a little in size with the density of the local population as dictated by the extent of arable land. Some of these villages have milk collection points from which it is brought to the central creameries for the making of butter. Some of these have been closed as the use of tractors and trucks extends feasible milk sheds, changing a pattern produced by the use of horses. The centripetal impetus of the switch from horses to cars and tractors over the past twenty years in this area has led to the concentration of some functions in fewer places. Continuing population loss till the mid-1960s also played a part. There is, however, a compensating centrifugal force in the area arising from tourists' desire for remoteness. Whereas thirty years ago only Tralee and Dingle had hotels, catering to the needs of salesmen, dealers and a few upper-class tourists, the peninsula is now liberally provided with hotels and guesthouses. The more remote west is especially attractive because Irish has survived there as a living language.

An even less complicated view of the effect of reducing distance friction on the fortunes of towns can be had on any route across the wheatlands of the Great Plains. There are the complications of rural depopulation taking its toll since the 1930s and the fact that settlements serve those in passage as well as the locals. Allowing for these effects, the centripetal effect is clearly visible in the human landscape. Travelling across west Kansas on U.S. 36, alongside branches of the Burlington and Rock Island Railroads, the grain elevators at ten-mile intervals mostly have pediments of boarded-up restaurants, hotels and shops, with a half-hearted, one-pump, gas station the only sign of life. The live towns with shops, John Deere and International Harvester dealers, truck stops, banks, new franchise eating places and motels, are at 40- to 50-mile intervals.

The Location of Material-Oriented Manufacturing

Several of the activities just discussed could be described as manufacturing, but they were treated as if the material they processed was distributed as the market was, or as if it was not costly to assemble. In either case, location with respect to the market is the touchstone of their fortunes. We can distinguish another form of manufacturing whose chief material input is specifically located, being a mineral outcrop or the product of another manufacturing process, and whose average costs decrease over the market range of our local economy. The location of such a regional, natural monopoly – if the demand for its product is pretty inelastic – is determined by the balance between assembly and distribution costs.

As an example we can consider the production of iron in our fictional economy and assume the price and quantity to be produced is fixed. The market is localized at the centre of the plain A, where tools are manufactured. One raw material, iron ore, is available at an outcrop located at F in figure 2.11, a distance D from the market. The other raw material is

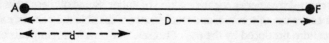

Figure 2.11

timber for charcoal. At the outset this is available everywhere at the same cost. Labour and capital cost the same no matter where they are employed. An entrepreneur interested in producing cast iron has, in this instance, only the location of the plant to decide about. With price and quantity given and all other costs the same, he would wish to locate his furnace in such a way as to minimize the cost of assembling the iron ore from F and distributing the product to A. As long as revenue exceeds outlays at some location, the transport-minimizing location will be the profit-maximizing one. His problem is to find a value for d, the distance of the furnace from the market in figure 2.11, where transport costs are minimized. Transport costs may be written:

$$aT_A(d)+bT_F(D-d)$$

where a is the freight rate per ton mile on the product and T_A is the tonnage required, and b the freight rate on iron ore and T_F the tonnage of ore required. If the production process is such that the raw material sheds weight in its transformation to its product, which would be the case with iron ore smelting, then $T_F > T_A$. Supposing the cost of transporting a ton of ore or iron were the same, i.e. $a = b$, then the iron-maker would seek to avoid as much iron ore carriage as possible and locate at F. To see this more clearly let us rewrite the transport cost expression in per unit product terms, letting C_A be the cost per mile for one ton of the product and C_F the cost of carrying for one mile enough ore to make one ton of the product:

UNIT TRANSPORT COST $= C_Ad+C_F(D-d)$

gathering terms we get: $(C_A-C_F)d+C_FD$. In this form we can see that when C_A is greater than C_F, the entrepreneur will keep d as small as possible and locate at the market A where d is zero. However, if the unit assembly costs C_F are greater than the unit distribution costs C_A, then the coefficient of d (i.e. (C_A-C_F)) will be negative and the iron-maker will want to locate at the maximum value of d, where $d = D$ at the material source F. Finally, if the cost of moving iron and iron ore are equal, so that $C_A = C_F$, the coefficient of d will be zero and transport costs will be C_FD wherever the furnace is located. The plant may then be located at A or F or any point between them.

In our iron-making case with a big weight loss involved and equal ton mile rates on materials and product, the material source would be the optimal location. Even if the transport rate were greater on the finished product, the weight loss involved in production may overwhelm this to make the material source more attractive. This is the force which has drawn the meat-packing industry further westwards in the U.S.A., first to Chicago in the 1870s and then to the centres of Missouri Valley stock-raising, Omaha and Kansas City. Even though rates per ton mile have favoured live animals over carcasses, the fact that the dressed meat of a steer weighs only 54 per cent of the live animal favours locations closer to material than market for slaughtering.

We have implied a very simple linear transport cost function in this discussion, while in Chapter 5 we will develop a much more elaborate version, with terminal costs and a tapering of cost with greater mileage. One set of terminal costs can usually be avoided by locating the production process at either the material source or the market. The tapering of cost per mile with distance similarly enhances end-points rather than intermediate locations, since it pays to carry either the material or the product as far as possible. Much of the world's productive capacity is, however, found at places intermediate between material sources and the centre of gravity of the material market – at ports. In moving between land and sea unavoidable transhipment costs are incurred. These costs of loading and unloading, and of the capital facilities used, must be borne no matter where the processing plant is located. If raw material is off-loaded straight over the dock into a processing plant and then the product is loaded straight onto the land carrier, clearly a set of loading and off-loading costs has been avoided compared with any other location than the material and market end-points. Given the relative costs of sea and land travel it is often advantageous to lose weight from the raw material before travelling over land. This is borne witness to by the concentration of oil-refining, paper-making, flour-milling, and increasing amounts of steel production alongside water. However, the existence of transhipment points reflects transport technology. Container and roll-on, roll-off traffic aimed at reducing transhipment costs will obviously reduce the advantage of ports as locations for manufacturing.

Most productive processes employ more than one non-ubiquitous raw material or intermediate good. To illustrate the effect of many sources we can invoke technical advance in our example and presume that the iron-maker learned that it is less costly to use coal for smelting. Suppose he finds a deposit of coal at C in figure 2.12 and wishes to proceed to combine 3 tons of coal and 2 tons of iron ore to produce 1 ton of iron to sell in A. Supposing that freight charges consist of 1 p/ton terminal costs and 1 p/ton/10 miles, being the same for coal, ore and iron. The iron-maker would

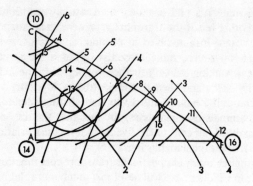

Figure 2.12

wish to find a location for his plant where the total transport bill is minimized. With three or more reference points there is now in effect a surface
of transport costs. At any point in the plain with grid coordinates (x_o, y_o),
the value of transport costs will be given by

$$T(x_o, y_o) = \sum_i a_i c_i d_{io}$$

where a_i is the weight of material i per unit of the product and is unity in
the case of the product itself, or a fraction representing the amount sold in
each market if there are several markets, c_i is the transport rate applicable
to good i and d_{io} is the distance from the source or market at $(x_i y_i)$ to $(x_o y_o)$.
  The producers' problem is to find the minimum point on this surface.
This cannot be done analytically, so a numerical solution is called for. To a
geographer the obvious solution would be to calculate the value of $T(x_o,y_o)$
for a sample of points in the triangle ACF and interpolate a contour map of
total transport costs. This surface can then be inspected to find its minimum
point. It is clear that this minimum must lie within the boundary joining
the sources and market. The total transport cost surface is constructed by
summing the assembly and distribution costs. In figure 2.12, lines of equal
transport cost for 3 tons of coal, 2 tons of iron ore and 1 ton of the product
are constructed about C, F, and A. These isotims are then summed to produce the surface of total cost, shown in the heavier lines. This isodapane
surface will form a saucer-like depression with its minimum point near the
centre, and thus suggesting an intermediate location. However, the surface
has three points of discontinuity, for at each of the corner points one set of
terminal costs can be avoided. Thus these corner points must be evaluated
separately and compared with the minimum point on the isodapane surface. The intermediate location at 13p per ton of product has lower costs

than F at 16p and A at 14p, but the source of coal with 10p per ton of iron beats out all other locations in minimizing assembly and distribution costs. Our example does reflect the historical conditions which drew the early iron and steel industry to the coalfields because of the enormous amount of coal required. As technology has reduced the amount of coal required so the pull of coal has relaxed, and the market, being also a source of the input scrap iron, has increased its pull. As the search for iron ore spanned the globe and its carriage became maritime, so coastal locations close to coal and markets became attractive. Gary, Indiana, does look like an intermediate location, but it is close to the centre of its market and it is a port situated where the lake system drives maritime traffic most deeply into the heart of the continent.

For this treatment we have assumed fixed inputs, allowing no substitution of materials and factors of production: we have assumed a monopolist who must accept both price and quantity as given; we have assumed consumers unresponsive to price; and we have also assumed perfect and certain knowledge of all these circumstances. The theory is probably best left in this simple form as a pedagogic device. It serves a purpose in explaining much of what we can observe in the world. We must, however, remember its limitations and keep in mind the proviso that the conditions it assumes do not usually obtain. In particular, it fails to treat the competitive jostling of a few large producers which characterizes heavy, material-oriented industry with decreasing costs. We will return to this question in the next chapter.

Labour and Land – Residential Rent and Density

The location of a single plant, mining coal and smelting iron, employing a fixed number of people on its own in the midst of farmland, provides an apt occasion for the following topic. The next concern is the land needs of an urban labour force for their dwellings, and how this works itself out in the economic landscape. Given the occupations and activities we have consigned to various settlements, we could expect them to have considerable populations both serving basic activities in their hinterland and as support providing for the needs of those engaged in basic production. The confusion of different skills, occupations and incomes of these central places complicates matters greatly. With the free-standing, integrated coal-mine and furnace located at C in figure 2.12 we have a simple setting in which to develop a theory.

Suppose the whole mining and iron-making activity needs manning in one twelve-hour shift of N people. A speculative builder buys land from farmers in the vicinity of the plant, unimaginatively divides it into N equal-sized plots clustered around the production site, and puts identical houses on them.

The supply curve of labour in figure 2.13 is generated by how much extra leisure a worker is willing to surrender for an increment of wages. This is the marginal value of leisure to the worker and slopes up to the right when

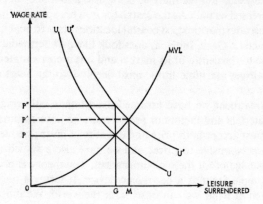

Figure 2.13

we plot leisure surrendered against the wage rate. We can assume the population to be uniform in these respects, so that the same curve represents the market reaction to changes in wages. The space between these axes will be structured by contour lines of equal income from combinations of wage rates and hours spent working. Combinations of wage rates and hours along uu will generate equal incomes, while a higher level of income is attainable by combinations along the locus $u'u'$. In order to induce people to forgo the twelve hours of the shift, OG, it would take a wage of OP per hour. However, all those workers at some remove from the work site have to give up a greater amount of leisure time than twelve hours, to the tune of the time it takes them to walk to work. If it takes the furthermost workers GM minutes to get to work, they would require a wage of OP' to induce them to work. The company, however, pays everybody the same wage for an OG hour day. To induce the marginal member of its required N man work force to come to work the firm would have to pay a rate of OP'' for an OG work day. This is the projection of the length of shift OG onto the equal income line $u'u'$ of the marginal worker with journey to work time GM. The same wage OP'' would have to be paid to all workers no matter what their location if the requisite number is to be attracted to work.

We can imagine that the sites and houses would be filled up from the plants outwards. The location of the furthermost workers and the time it takes them to get to work determines the wage paid to all. Obviously those closer to work are getting a bonus over and above their supply price and it is equal to the difference in travel time between theirs, and the furthermost worker's, valued at the marginal value of leisure. This bonus is at a maximum for those who live right beside the works and who spend no time in walking.

This advantage accrues in money and the builder will be able to charge rents which capture this value. We may imagine the rental charged to be composed of two parts. There is firstly a fixed charge for the facilities of the house and to cover the alternative use of the land in agriculture. This latter value may be considered constant for present purposes, since we are dealing with a very small ambit compared to that over which agricultural rent varies significantly. The second part of the rental is a variable charge equal to the difference in journey-to-work costs between any location and the furthermost houses from the place of work. This value is at a maximum at the plant and declines to zero at the margin. These charges can be levied since, if there is competition among workers for houses, it would pay someone further out to bid a higher rent for a closer house up to the point where rents equal travel cost differentials. Only at that juncture would everyone be indifferent between locations. Rents thus equalize workers' net incomes. We can view the wage paid OP'' as consisting of a pure shift-time payment plus rent plus journey-to-work costs. The level of the total wage is determined by the travel cost of the marginal workers, whose location rent approaches zero. This familiar structure of rents declining with increasing inaccessibility operates to compensate for the advantage of relative location. That urban land values do indeed take on this pattern of decrease from the centre out is illustrated by a map of land value per acre for Topeka, Kansas, in 1956, figure 2.14.

The population density in the circumstances we have described is uniform. This was determined by the developer's original layout. The implicit assumption of a uniform density was that the demand for space was perfectly inelastic; that everyone was happy with the same amount of room, no matter the price. Now suppose that the demand for space is responsive to price, so that more space will be consumed at a lower price per square yard. In the longer run as our town sorts itself out, those who live closer in and who pay more rent per square yard are likely to adjust their consumption downward whenever the opportunity arises – by sub-letting, for example. The developer, as he replaces the modified buildings, can increase the density of population closer in by putting more dwellings on the same area by means of flats, less open space, etc. At the same time, the con-

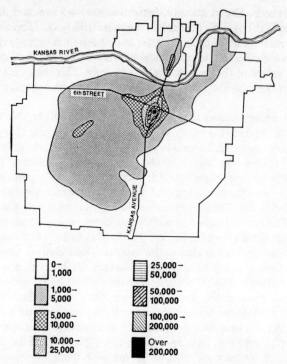

KANSAS RIVER

6th STREET

KANSAS AVENUE

0–1,000	25,000–50,000
1,000–5,000	50,000–100,000
5,000–10,000	100,000–200,000
10,000–25,000	Over 200,000

Figure 2.14 After Duane S. Knos, 'The Distribution of Land Values in Topeka, Kansas', University of Kansas, Bureau of Business and Economic Research, pp. 15–33, figure 1.

sumption of space at lower prices per square yard of peripheral positions is likely to rise. With adjustments to the building stock more open space will be provided and lots will be aggregated, tending to reduce population density. The overall outcome will be the often-remarked tendency for residential density to decline with distance from the centre. This phenomenon we experience in our everyday travels is not just a matter of the history of tastes in living space nor of differences in income but, as we have seen, can be generated by journey-to-work cost differences and a downward-sloping demand curve for space with a uniform population.

When we introduce an elasticity of demand for room into the picture, the equilibrium of the market is less simple to determine. Density, or the inverse of the amount of land consumed per capita, will vary with the price per square yard of land. This decreases from the work-place to the edge of the town. Thus, density will in general decrease from the centre to the edge, where it will become zero. This gives us a cone-like surface as in figure 2.15. The volume under this density surface will have to equal N households, if we assume one worker per household. The position of the marginal households, upon which the structure of rents depends, can be determined by

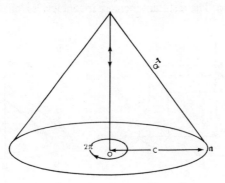

Figure 2.15

finding the travel cost distance (c) over which it is necessary to spread the density cone by raising its axis, in order to obtain a total population N. Mathematically, we wish to find the limit of integration (n), necessary for a negatively inclined density function (Q^{-1}), rotated about a central axis (2π) to describe a volume of N. N can be written

$$N = 2\pi \int_0^n (Q^{-1})dc$$

and the unknown to be solved for in our case is n. Once the distance c at n has been determined, then the travel-cost differences between that location and all others will yield the rent every household pays for their accommodation. Having fixed n, we know the density at every distance from the centre. This, multiplied by the total rent, will give the rent per square yard.

We can imagine this simple construction elaborated in recognition of the non-Euclidean features of geographical space, replacing 2π by a mapping function between Euclidean space and transport networks space. The single purpose could be replaced by several urban land uses such as retailing, manufacturing, and by different income and social classes with different space preferences. Bid-rent functions could be constructed after the fashion of our discussion of agricultural uses, and competition between uses could be treated. However, even without these realistic elaborations, the simplest formulation does give us the wherewithal to understand much we can see when applied to changed circumstances.

If the demand for iron increased and the desired amount of labour increases, in the short term a higher wage would attract more labour to the edge of the existing town and extend the margin of settlement from n_1 to n_2 in figure 2.16a. The resultant increase in rent levels from R_1 to R_2 will in

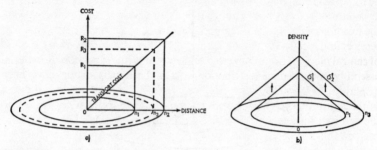

Figure 2.16

the longer run lead to an adjustment in density conditions with people consuming less space. Densities will increase everywhere in the town and the margin of occupation may shrink to n_3 – reducing the rent levels to R_3. In reality, this tendency has often been offset by decreasing transport costs as technology reduces the friction of distance. Suppose that bicycles or buses are introduced to our workers. If wages remain fixed, as the innovation rotates the cost of travel down from c_1 to c_2 in figure 2.17a, so the margin of feasibility is extended from n_1 to n_2. A greater amount of space would be available to the same population. The resulting longer-term density adjustments would take the form of a reduction of density closer in and an increase in density at the extending edge of the town as in figure 2.17b. The actual path of density and extent of residential land use has been a response

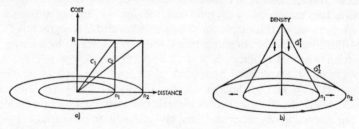

Figure 2.17

to these countervailing forces of population growth and reduction in distance friction, with the latter prevailing.

Conclusion

With an extremely simple theory of residential land use, we have completed a sketch of the chief components of the economic landscape which bears some resemblance to our experience of its arrangement. The value of agricultural land has been established in its relation to transport costs and the location of the market. The geographical market shares of providers of services and locally-used manufactures have been established as a structure of central places. The pulls exerted on heavy industry's location by material assembly and product distribution cost and their balancing have been displayed. At the most local level, we have seen the way in which the cost of the journey to work structures both the map of urban land values and the density of residential uses. In all of these cases, a close connection has been established between the value of land or a location and accessibility, i.e. the advantages of a site in terms of avoiding transport costs in serving a given purpose.

Readings

The seed for location theory was sown by J. H. von Thünen in 1826. This is available in translation by C. Wartenberg as *The isolated state*, Pergamon, London, 1966. His analysis is extended and presented in more recent terms by E. S. Dunn, 'The equilibrium of land use patterns in agriculture', *Southern Economic Journal*, no. 21, 1955, pp. 173–87. Similar but distinct theories of central places were elaborated independently by a geographer, W. Christaller, in 1933, translated by C. W. Baskin as *Central places in South Germany*, Prentice Hall, Englewood Cliffs, N.J., 1966, and an economist, A. Losch, in 1940, translated by W. H. Woglom as *The economics of location*, Yale University Press, New Haven, Conn., 1954.

These works are summarized, along with a mass of empirical evidence for regularity, by B. J. L. Berry, *Geography of market centers and retail distribution*, Prentice Hall, Englewood Cliffs, N.J., 1967.

The foundation of industrial location theory was laid by A. Weber whose work is available in translation by C. J. Friedrich as *Alfred Weber's theory of location of industries*, University of Chicago Press, Chicago, 1929. More recent developments are described by D. Smith in *Industrial location*, Wiley, London, 1971.

The theory of residential land use and rent derives from von Thünen's construction and has been variously embellished by Lowdon Wingo Jr,

Transportation and Urban Land, Washington, D.C., Resources for the Future, 1961. W. Alonso, *Location and land use*, Harvard University Press, Cambridge, Mass., 1964, and R. F. Muth, *Cities and housing*, University of Chicago Press, Chicago, 1969.

3. Geographical Competition

In our discussion in the last chapter of producers' behaviour in geographical space, assumptions of many producers and free entry by new producers were employed to warrant perfectly competitive resolution of market prices and quantities. On the other hand, to investigate industrial plant location, the other extreme of a natural monopolist, bound by government regulation as to price and quantity output, was invoked. This reduced the problem to a cost-minimizing one. What we often see about us lies between these extremes. Frequently, it is a matter of a few large producers jostling for a national market, constrained to some degree by government control, real or potential. This is the case with the manufacture of cars, beer, processed foods, inter-city travel, television and newspapers. The behaviour of such oligopolists becomes a ceaseless game with no predictable outcome. It is impossible to determine a market equilibrium in such competitive circumstances and thus to judge whether it is socially desirable. There is a contention that, in general, oligopolistic competition leads to excessive similarity of products, which is not in accord with the best interests of all of society. In geographical terms, this centripetal force takes the form of locating production in the same place. More generally, it involves closing the spectrum of product type and quality on offer. The debate on this issue has usually been couched in terms of the geography of production. This is so because the physical distance and transport cost separation between producers is a simple dimension along which to measure their dissimilarity. The underlying concern, however, is with the general question of product similarity. A geographical setting with two producers competing for a market spread evenly along a line, in the familiar form of ice-cream sellers on a beach, is a well-defined simplification with which to attack the general issue.

Duopolistic Competition for a Linear Market

The source of instability in treating of duopolistic competition is the fact that, if customers select either of two sellers on the basis of price difference alone, they will swing entirely from one to the other with the opening up of any price difference. The outcome of competition will depend on the expectation of each seller as to the other seller's reaction to his changing price or output. The outcome of such games is a matter of tactics and not the resultant of forces leading inevitably to a unique state of rest. There are, however, other reasons than a price difference for buying from one seller rather than another. There are qualitative and sentimental reasons which generate a degree of local monopoly for a seller. Perhaps the most powerful reason for such localized market hegemony is the cost of overcoming distance. Due to distance friction every seller has a potential for geographical monopoly power. The price difference between two sellers must exceed any additional transport costs incurred from the switch in order to induce a change in patronage. With this limited degree of monopoly power, changes are no longer catastrophic but can be envisaged as occurring continuously as the price gap between competitors opens up. If we introduce a geographical dimension to competition, removing the market from a pinhead and allowing for more than one price prevailing, then the seeming instability of duopolistic competition can be reduced to a balanced outcome.

Suppose that two mobile fish-and-chip shops serving an extensive market in South Wales coincide in their rounds once a week in one village. This settlement consists of a mile-long single row of houses evenly strung out along a narrow valley. On any one service day each vendor can select any location along the street. Having selected a site and set up shop there, they must stay there for the duration of the day. On the day of this visit every household buys one order of fish and chips, patronizing the shop with the lowest delivered price. The delivered price is made up of the price of an order at the shop plus the cost of going to the shop, valued at say c pence per furlong by all villagers. We can picture the market by the line in figure 3.1 with its eight-furlong divisions numbered from north to south. With

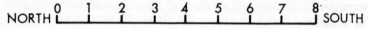

Figure 3.1

similar and constant production costs per order, the two shop-owners will make their price and location decisions in terms of maximizing revenue. Their share of this uniform mile-long market is determined by the boundary of indifference between them. This is drawn where the customers perceive delivered prices to be the same. Thus, for each competitor, the location of this boundary will depend on the price the other seller charges.

At the outset of their battle, suppose they located one at the northern extreme and the other at the southern end of the village and sought to maximize their revenue from those positions. Each would have an incentive to decrease price until he controlled half the market extending to the centre of the village at furlong 4, supposing this price more than covered costs. To cut price further would simply bring a similar reaction from the other seller, maintaining market shares at a loss of revenue. Thus the equilibrium prices and quantities would be equal for the two shops.

It would eventually strike one of the vendors that he could increase his market share and revenue at the same price by moving towards the centre of the village. Say the northern vendor decides one week to set up at the second furlong. If, as he expected, the southern seller sets up at the far extremity of the village, furlong 8, as usual, he can capture five furlongs of the market at the equilibrium price. This is because the villagers, if they perceive distance differences precisely as they step out of their doorways, will be indifferent between the two shops at the five furlong mark. Predicting that the northern seller will return to furlong 2 for the next visit, the southern seller can capture back his original share and more of the market by moving deeper into it than the northern seller did. Say he moves to the mid-point at furlong 4. The line of indifference will then lie at the third furlong, the northern seller retaining only three furlongs of the village as opposed to the other's five furlongs. It is evident to the intuition that the end result of this locational tussle will be reached when the northern seller also locates at the mid-point furlong 4 and the two divide the market and revenue equally, standing back to back. The mathematical exposition of this argument is given in the appendix to this chapter.

The balance between the two at this location, arising from a privately motivated competitive process, is at odds with the best interests of the villagers. Central location does not represent a social optimum. The social costs involved in this case are the transport costs of going to the shops. These will plainly be lowest when the shops divide the market between them by locating at the second and sixth furlong, i.e. the quartile points. The maximum one-way trip anyone will incur will be two furlongs and the total transport costs will be $8c$ pence. However, the competitive urge prompting these duopolists will prevent them from stopping at this socially desirable juncture and drive them towards the centre of the village. There the transport costs of the villagers are greater. The longest trip will be four furlongs now and the total transport cost will be doubled at $16c$ pence.

This contention, that the equilibrium arising from oligopolistic competition is socially sub-optimal, has been used as a prescriptive stick to beat private locational decisions of firms and justify stringent control of industrial location in the U.K. via Industrial Development Certificates and Development Area legislation. The originator of the argument, H.

Hotelling, did not deny that there are economies associated with central clustering, the agglomeration economies we shall turn to in the next chapter. Nevertheless he held that competition among a few producers led to concentration in excess of that justified by these agglomeration economies. A superficial glance at the coincidence of branch plants in Los Angeles, California, and Tampa, Florida, of two of the major brewers of the U.S.A., Schlitz and Anheuser-Busch, who account for 35 per cent of the national market between them, is suggestive of this tendency.

Sensitivity to Prices, Transport Costs, and Market Shares

The above conclusion, that a loss of social welfare arises from the balance of oligopolists' private interests, is based on an assumption of infinite elasticity of demand and precise perception of travel cost differences by buyers. If these assumptions are dropped and if the geographical framework is extended from a line to a circular plane, an opposite centrifugal tendency can be rationalized. A more general geographic context is provided by the circular isotropic market of uniform consumer density employed in the last two chapters. Let us assume that two sellers provide an identical good to this market at a fixed price. They vary their sales by varying their location. We may suppose that their locational game is played in mirror image of each other, along a given axis of the plain at points like a

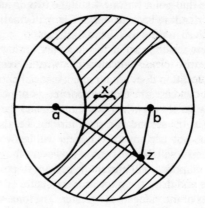

Figure 3.2

and b in figure 3.2. We will retain the axiom that consumers behave in an economically consistent manner and patronize the nearest vendor. In doing this, however, there is some minimum distance, say ten yards (x in figure 3.2), below which they do not perceive a difference in distance to be important. If, on stepping out of their doorway, customers glance up and down, and the difference between going to the northern or southern shops is less than ten yards, they will be indifferent between going to one or the other. The difference in distance to the buyers is inconsequential. The existence of such minimum sensible thresholds of sensitivity has been remarked in human reactions to a wide range of phenomena and must appeal to our sense of how we approximate solutions to everyday problems. We do habitually use a three-valued logic and have a 'maybe' category of indifference between 'yes' and 'no'. In the area of indifference, customers will not necessarily split evenly between two sellers in any market time period. They may be influenced by herding instincts. If, on stepping out, you meet a neighbour going one way, you would be more inclined to join them and this can accumulate to all of those in the indifference range going one way.

In addition to the limit of sensitivity to transport costs, we can introduce sensitivity to price in terms of how much people buy. We can propose a more usual downward-sloping demand curve for fish and chips, say, so that as delivered price increases, demand tapers off. Under these conditions, the sellers must take both their market share and also total sales into account in making their decisions. Lower delivered prices mean higher sales and more revenue for everyone. Sales and profits can be increased either by securing a larger share of a given market *or* by increasing total sales with the same share *or* by some combination of both. Under a fixed shop price, total sales will vary with the locational configuration of the sellers and the locational changes which, with correspondingly lower transport costs for the community, will release purchasing power, thereby increasing total sales of the product.

The market boundaries between locations a and b with a sensitivity threshold will be the locus of points, such as z in figure 3.2, where the difference between distances az and bz is a constant equal to x (10 yards in our example) i.e. $|az-bz| = x$. These loci turn out to be hyperbolas focused on a and b, so that the area of indifference between the monopolized markets of a and b is a hyperbolic fan, as shown by the shaded area in figure 3.2. As the competitors get closer together, so that zone of indifference gets larger as in figure 3.3. When the distance from a to b is less than x, the sensitivity threshold, the hyperbolas, collapse. The difference between going to either shop becomes a matter of no consequence for the whole market. Each seller can only count on the possible patronage of everyone in general and hence of no one in particular. As the duopolists move apart along the axis, the area of indifference wanes. In the limiting case of peripheral location the area of uncertainty becomes a radial section of

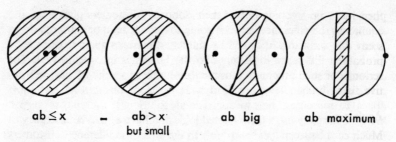

ab ≤ x   –   ab > x·   ab big   ab maximum
                 but small

Figure 3.3

width x. At these polar locations on the axis each seller is most assured of his maximum market share, just less than half of the total. Now uncertainty about the size of sales is costly. Even if, over the long pull, half the buyers go to each shop when they are located at the centre, for each weekly visit of our chip shop, say, it cannot be assured of the sales it will enjoy. To cater for this it will have to increase the stocks it holds to satisfy – possibly - the entire market once in a while, as buyers switch backwards and forwards in a capricious fashion. Costs of stock are kept to a minimum by having a reliable stream of customers. This could induce the competitors to move apart, reducing the area of uncertainty and, thereby, the inventory costs involved.

If the competitors go to the extreme of polar location to reduce uncertainty and stock costs, they maximize the risk of a third competitor coming between them and stripping them both of a large share of their monopoly power. This is the most risky, if most certain, strategy as far as the market is concerned.

With both polar and central locations, the transport costs of the customers are at their highest. Departure either outwards from the centre or inwards from the circumference of the market will result in reductions in travel costs and delivered price, increases in disposable income for the customer and thus in total sales of the product in question. At two points part-way between the centre and edge of the market, like a and b in figure 3.2, the average distance travelled is minimized. For a circular market these two points are approximately two-fifths of the length of the radius from the centre. Location at these points minimizes total travel cost and maximizes total sales. Depending on the trade-off between lowering inventory costs, increasing total sales and opening up the centre of the market to a third entrant, some position between the extremes seems attractive. If the centripetal urge to exclude new entrants is small and the centrifugal influence of inventory costs is balanced by the merit of increasing total sales, then location at the points of minimum travel may be the competitive equilibrium. From this balance of motives the central clustering solution seems the most unlikely and location at the socially optimal points most probable. Thus, given quite reasonable assumptions about behaviour, serious doubt can be cast on the simple conclusion of social and competitive disparity expounded previously.

Agglomeration

Much of the observable clustering of production and service is a response to the strong central tendency in the disposition of population and activities as a whole. The aforementioned pairing of locations from which Schlitz and Bud are dispensed to California and Florida in Los Angeles and Tampa is not surprising when you examine the distribution of the population in those states. In Chapter 6 it will be proposed that this clustering of population is a response to scale economies involved in providing a transport network. Starting from a plain of uniform density, the most efficient network structure will radiate out from the centre. The implied deformation of the accessibility surface encourages an intensification of activities and population at the centre of the plain and the urban clusters most of us inhabit. The next chapter, 4, will take up the story of the advantages of closeness more generally.

Appendix

Competition for a Linear Marketing

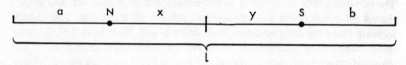

Figure 3.4

Let two producers N and S with zero costs of production vie for a uniformly dense linear market of length l with perfectly inelastic demand for one unit of the product per unit length of the line in any market period. Customers transport the good from the producers' locations to their home at a cost of c per unit distance. They patronize the seller with the lowest delivered price, taking transport cost as well as F.O.B. price into account. Producer N locates at a distance a from the northern end of the market and the market boundary will be at a distance x from him. S is b distance from the opposite end and at a remove of y from the market dividing line. The market boundary represents the point of customer indifference between N and S. If p_N is N's price and p_S that of S, x and y, and thus market shares, can be determined by putting the delivered prices of the two sellers equal:

$$p_N + cx = p_S + cy.$$

We have defined x and y to be related so that:

$$a + x + y + b = l$$

so that we can solve for x and y

$$x = \tfrac{1}{2}\left(l - a - b + \frac{p_S - p_N}{c}\right)$$

and

$$y = \tfrac{1}{2}\left(l - a - b + \frac{p_N - p_S}{c}\right).$$

With zero production costs, profit for the two sellers will be the product of price and quantity sold, which in this case is the length of the market monopolized:

$$\Pi_N = p_N(a+x) = \tfrac{1}{2}(l+a-b)p_N - \frac{p_N{}^2}{2c} + \frac{p_N p_S}{2c}$$

$$\Pi_S = p_S(b+y) = \tfrac{1}{2}(l-a+b)p_S - \frac{p_S{}^2}{2c} + \frac{p_N p_S}{2c}.$$

The two sellers will adjust their prices so as to maximize these profits, given the price the other charges. They will increase their prices until the rate of increase of profits becomes zero. This point is found by taking the partial derivative of the profit function with respect to price and equating that to zero and solving for price. Taking the partials for the two profit expressions and setting them to zero we obtain:

$$\frac{\partial \Pi_N}{\partial p_N} = \frac{l+a-b}{2} - \frac{p_N}{c} + \frac{p_S}{2c} = 0$$

and

$$\frac{\partial \Pi_S}{\partial p_S} = \frac{l-a+b}{2} + \frac{p_N}{2c} - \frac{p_S}{c} = 0.$$

These can be solved to find the prices such that neither seller can increase profits by changing his price:

$$p^N = c\left(l + \frac{a-b}{3}\right)$$

$$p_S = c\left(l - \frac{a-b}{3}\right).$$

The market interval monopolized by each gives the equilibrium quantities sold:

$$q_N = a+x = \tfrac{1}{2}\left(l + \frac{a-b}{3}\right)$$

$$q_S = b+y = \tfrac{1}{2}\left(l - \frac{a-b}{3}\right).$$

To this point the sellers have remained stationary at a and b from the ends of the market. We now turn to location as variable in the contest. Supposing that there are no costs associated with relocation and locational costs are everywhere the same, we can obtain the relation between location and profits by putting the equilibrium values of price and quantity into the expressions for profit:

$$\Pi_N = \tfrac{1}{2}c\left(l+\frac{a-b}{3}\right)^2$$

$$\Pi_S = \tfrac{1}{2}c\left(l-\frac{a-b}{3}\right)^2.$$

The location decision variables are a and b. From these expressions it is obvious that to maximize profits N must maximize a and S must maximize b, and thus that they will end up located together at the centre of the market.

At this competitive equilibrium the social cost involved is the total transport bill, which is given by:

$$\text{TRANSPORT COST} = \tfrac{1}{2}c(a^2+b^2+x^2+y^2).$$

If we let l equal unity, then for this central location this is:

$$= \tfrac{1}{2}c|(\tfrac{1}{2})^2+(\tfrac{1}{2})^2| = \frac{c}{4}.$$

This is clearly more than the transport cost generated by location at the socially optimal quartile points where the transport expenditure is:

$$= \tfrac{1}{2}c|(\tfrac{1}{4})^2+(\tfrac{1}{4})^2+(\tfrac{1}{4})^2+(\tfrac{1}{4})^2| = \frac{c}{8}.$$

Readings

The classical piece on spatial competition is H. Hotelling, 'Stability in competition', *Economic Journal*, no. 39, 1929, pp. 41–57. There is a more recent counterpoint to this by N. Devletoglou, 'A dissenting view of duopoly and spatial competition', *Economica,* May 1965, pp. 140–60.

4. Agglomeration Economies

One influence shaping the economic landscape has not been given proper attention up to this point. The economies of agglomeration have been referred to in passing or dismissed by assumption. In the last chapter it was suggested that central clustering may arise from a search for these advantages rather than from any competitive urge drawing oligopolists towards the centre of a market. The evidence from our experience of the use of the land is of a massive degree of concentration of competing and complementary activities, pointing to a most potent force. Observation suggests that some industries derive advantages from locating in major centres of production or consumption, or from close association with other units of the same industry. The degrees of conglomeration in the geographical distribution of different activities point to a varying response to these agglomerative forces. To sort these matters out it will be necessary to be a little more specific. The advantages which give rise to industrial concentration have been recognized as powerful, yet are held difficult to evaluate. The main reason is that 'agglomeration economies' is a blanket term applied indiscriminately to a variety of specific advantages arising from proximate location.

Looking at maps of industrial production and plant locations for clues as to the nature of agglomeration economies must be done with historical perspective. The landscape we see has in it elements reflecting past technological, economic and political conditions. In examining changes in the distribution of activities it is important to avoid confusing changes in the evaluation of distance over time with positive forces leading to dispersion. Geographical interaction is not governed by mere distance, but by the cost of movement. This is a temporal, as well as a spatial, variable. A decrease in the cost of movement over time, reducing the friction of distance, may permit a change in the scale of concentration, yet the advantages of concentration are still enjoyed to the same extent. The five-mile radius of a viable metropolis in the 1830s, evidenced by London's ring of main-line railway stations, has been extended to fifty in the last century and a half and Inter-City 125 now stretches commuter land to the Cotswolds. The greatest growth of company headquarter offices in the U.S.A. is to be found in Fairfield County, Connecticut, lying thirty to sixty miles from Manhattan in Greenwich, Stamford, Darien, Westpoint, Fairfield and Danbury. In 1968 the county had only four of *Fortune*'s top 500 companies. In 1978 it had 24, being tied with Chicago for second place after New York City's 82. Such changes in the scale of concentration permitted by transport technology cannot be considered a positive tendency towards dispersal.

The economic question which arises is concerned with variation in costs and revenue. What is it about the concentration of manufacturing activities in certain places which could possibly lead to higher returns to factor inputs than might alternative arrangements? From the distribution of human activities, even in areas of fairly homogeneous resource availability, it appears that there are great advantages to be had from congregating in particular places. Manufacturing is mainly urban. The existence of industrial belts, metropolis and megalopolis in which most manufacturing is concentrated, points to some economy. Prior to the introduction of ordnance to warfare, clustered settlement presented a defensive advantage. Now, with airborne explosive power, the military motive would favour dispersal. Since there seems no logical negative reason for the huddling of activities, there must be some positive factors bringing it about. The advantages of specialization and division of labour are the most important of these. In terms of processing costs, the higher efficiency lies in concentration. This influence is counterbalanced by the resistance offered to the gathering of raw materials and distribution of final products by distance, measured in terms of transport costs. Out of this balance come distribution patterns which differ from industry to industry and which change with technical innovations and tastes affecting one or the other side of the balance.

Scale Economies

As the first element of agglomeration economies let us examine internal economies of concentration. One of the reasons for concentrated production is the existence of scale economies of production. Clearly, the larger the prevalent size of the plant, the larger the market it can serve, the fewer the locations it is necessary to occupy, the more concentrated is production. These economies of scale arise from the advantages of division of labour and specialization and are partly technological in nature. Specialization and the application of specialized capital equipment to production leads to a greater output at a lower cost in terms of resources used up. The lowest cost per unit product of specialized capital is frequently very large. The technologically ideal steel plant of the 1970s would produce 4 million tons of steel per annum, with 3 million tons rolling off the mill as final product and one million tons of scrap recycling to combine with 3 million tons of pig-iron as the steel furnace charge. This large optimum size severely limits the number of significant production locations.

Further savings can be achieved by buying and selling in large quantities and spreading management and supervision overheads over a large number of units of output. However, the degree of specialization and concentration is limited by the size of the market. Generally, even if resources were uniformly spread over the land, the efficiency of large-scale production would draw some forms of production to a limited number of localities. In fact resources are not evenly spread and the centres of concentration which emerge are places with natural or acquired advantages of some kind to offer industry.

Integration Economies

Closely related to scale economies, there are economies of integrated processes which lead to the agglomeration of several manufacturing processes in one plant. Examples of such economies are the heat savings from transferring molten pig-iron to steel furnaces; the use of coke-oven waste gases in hot blasts for steel furnaces; the minimization of movement and heating costs by the juxtaposition of steel furnaces, slabbing and rolling mills, and the recycling of internal scrap in an integrated steel works. The minimization of transfer costs by the use of a continuous assembly line in car manufacturing is perhaps the most complete integration. Such an integration of processes demands production on a very large scale in order that each separate unit of production is kept operating economically. The individual components of the production process will have at least to be in multiples sufficient to serve the minimum efficient size of the largest component of the process. In steel production this was the rolling or slabbing mill. Since the introduction of the Linz-Donawitz and Kaldo converters in the 1960s, it has been the steel furnace which sets the scale.

External Economies of Agglomeration

There are economies connected with the geographical association of plants of the same or different industries which are external to the decision-making firm.

Firstly, what have been entitled *linkage economies* are not far removed from the economies of integration. The concentration of separate works pursuing the same kind of process or participating in a sequence of operations is a common feature of industrial distribution. The benefits given rise to by this type of grouping include the economy of specialization of an individual firm in one particular process linked in a chain of production. This permits the adoption of specialized techniques and capital that would not be possible in an individual small-scale plant attempting to pursue the whole sequence within its own walls. Such linked or related industries often require similar types of labour skill and there is room, therefore, for a high degree of labour mobility, which is to the advantage of economic efficiency. A further advantage is easy interchange of materials and products between linked establishments, facilitated by proximity. The road can be used as a conveyor belt. Moving material by truck or porter from one small plant to another, as in the clothes industry, may be cheaper than movement within a large factory by conveyor belt. There are in addition certain specialized and general services often associated with linked industries, and these afford considerable economy in the maintenance and service staffs of individual firms. It is typical of such industrial environments that some small firms will specialize in processes rather than in products. They can undertake a variety of specialized work 'put-out' by others. They are flexible in operation, and able to change materials or designs according to requirements at short notice. Close relationships between related firms, able to meet without inconvenience, reduce further the costs of distance.

Three common types of linkage have been distinguished. Vertical linkage is the connection of separate firms, each performing one of a series of operations. In the non-ferrous metal trades of the West Midlands, the sequence is from metal refining to metal shaping, to manufacturing, to finishing. Horizontal linking describes the relation of firms whose different products are assembled into a final product. The component manufacturers upon which the car industry draws to assemble its product exemplify this structure. Diagonal association implies that a firm produces a good or service that is required at various stages in the production process. Firms providing tools for other plants, or specializing in processes such as stamping or piercing, are said to link diagonally with other firms.

The economies which arise from these types of association may be so great that new entrants to an industry have little choice. Location near the established clustering may be a precondition of success. The social relationships among linked firms at the main concentration may make it difficult for a newcomer in another location to obtain regular and reliable orders. The micro-electronics industry has taken on such a pattern since its birth in 1963, with 500 firms clustered in Santa Clara County's 'Silicon Valley', forty miles south of San Francisco.

Along with the economies of linkage in a concentrated and specialized industrial area, there are frequently *communal economies* associated with the development of many essential services tailored to the needs of the main industries. In Nordrhein-Westfalen the development of a gas grid, using coke-oven and blast-furnace waste gases, has led to considerable economy in power of the area. This is of advantage to the chemical industry and also to the iron and steel industry, since the grid acts as a clearing house, evening out surfeits and deficits of power. In Lorraine, the steel companies and Electricité de France have a similar arrangement. Other communal advantages include banking and insurance facilities geared to local needs, the availability of short-term capital, marketing facilities, and middlemen, maintenance and repair services designed for particular industrial needs. Transport services are frequently adapted to specific requirements, often offering special rates because of a large volume of traffic. Educational services, especially technical colleges and evening institutions, may direct themselves to the training requirements of local industries. Research organizations and information circulated in trade journals are important communal advantages, though they need no longer exert a powerful geographic localizing force. However, the prestige and advertising advantages of a location in the large established centres with high reputations are a tremendous attraction. For a cutlery or high-speed steel producer to locate outside the Sheffield area would be to put itself at a serious disadvantage, since 'Sheffield' is synonymous with such products.

Urban Economies

All of these communal economies are related to the economies of urbanization and what has been termed geographical inertia. People and production tend to congregate in urban places because this leads to a maximization of returns to effort. A basic cost in human activity is that involved in overcoming distance. Towns exist because of the proximity of man to man, for convenience of contact and exchange. Space offers a positive disutility which is a joint product of distance, the means of overcoming it and the importance of contact to the activity involved. The desire to overcome the cost of contact is a most potent economic force. The geography of the economy is the resultant of the desire to minimize the cost of contact and the fact that our activities inherently require space for their execution. Urban concentrations are an effort to minimize frictional costs by maximizing accessibility. A town is a peak in the field of market potential and customer convenience. It is the most convenient point for the assembly of materials, becoming the centre for employment opportunity and thus for the supply of factors of production, labour, capital and management. Urban locations are attractive because they offer low costs and high returns for production and consumption. The large, fluid urban labour market offers a wide range of skills from people attracted to the city by its comparative advantages for consumption, opportunity and social and cultural life. A concentration of opportunities also attracts entrepreneurial skill. Agglomeration in a city presents opportunities for specialization and the advantages derived from large-scale, more efficient, production. Such advantages of scale and specialization apply equally to social and cultural facilities, even though their provision is often a collective matter and not priced in a market. Greater and better output can be achieved at lower cost than could be achieved by individuals or small communities satisfying their own needs. The prestige of a city and its reputation for success are real attractive forces for industry based on sensible reactions, for reputations for success are not won easily. For industries whose fortunes are tied to technical advance, the universities, technical institutes, libraries and laboratories of great cities still exert a pull, though it is diminishing with improvements in communications.

The advantages cited as agglomeration economies derive from the process of growth. Some towns have continued to grow as industrial centres despite the disappearance of the locational impulse which first gave momentum to their growth, frequently the existence of mineral resources. This effect is labelled geographic inertia. But to say that the deposits of carboniferous coal and black band ores in the West Midlands precipitated industrial development there is to over-simplify. The utility of mineral deposits is measured in terms of their accessibility and the market for them. Many areas whose early development exploited mineral wealth, such as the Black Country, were also at the heart of large market areas. Even without the Ruhr coalfield, the junction of the Rhine and the Börde possesses many advantages for industrial development. Chicago is a mighty industrial complex with no coal or metal ore croppings but at the hub of U.S. internal transport, witnessing the potency of market accessibility alone. Wyoming, with its vast reserves of low sulphur coal, shows little potential for massive industrial development, being removed from major markets. The decline in activity of less accessible areas of mineral production, such as the Superior Uplands or the north-east coalfield of England, when their mineral deposits become depleted, is a clear sign of this.

This aside, once development is under way, the acquired advantages of a particular locale are every bit as real as the presence of fuel or metals. Capital equipment, being highly immobile, since it represents a large investment which cannot readily be written off, often prevents immediate readjustment to small changes in the balance of other locational advantages. The fact that it can be less costly to expand production *in situ* than in a green-field site has a similar effect. These inertial effects can represent real advantage. It may be that the other disadvantages of some existing location are more than offset by the saving in capital expenditures of building elsewhere. A pathological situation arises when the level of returns to capital at an existing location are kept artificially high by manipulating the market mechanism or by legislation. This prevents the efficient transfer of production to better alternative locations. The Pittsburgh Plus pricing system for steel in the U.S.A., which held sway from 1900 till 1924, was such an attempt and did retard the growth of output at the southern end of Lake Michigan and in Birmingham, Alabama. The immobility of a skilled labour force sentimentally attached to an area is another such force of momentum for continued growth. The development of transport, public utility and social infrastructure, not least a stock of housing, is a further impetus to incremental growth in an existing agglomeration rather than starting afresh. It is, however, reasonable to postulate that the major regions which enjoy and maintain these acquired advantages have the underlying advantage of centrality, and would not have so developed if they had not had this advantage.

Efficient Land Use and Optimum City Size

People and activities have congregated in urban centres to reduce distance friction. The residual frictional costs are reflected in land rents and transport costs. Each land user seeks a site for which his friction costs are minimized and is willing to pay a rent which, when added to the transport costs associated with the location, is just less than the total of rent and transport costs for alternative locations. In a competitive land market the most efficient user of a particular parcel, who can make the most of its aggregate of convenience in carrying out his operations, will outbid all others. Given the interplay of various land users as competitors, complements, producers and consumers whose tastes and technology change, there is a constant shifting of land occupancies. This market process is subject to imperfections but it does offer an approximation to the value the community places on various locational conveniences expressed through effective demand. In extending the urban margin out to some radius it gives concrete expression to the limit of efficient agglomeration.

Many hold that the shortcomings of the market involved and especially its failure to signal external costs to users have led to cities of excessive size. It is argued that the large city with its lengthy daily work trips wastes resources. The populations of the largest cities have exceeded the optimum and many are now subject to diminishing returns as the external costs of congestion in traffic, pollutants and social alienation mount. This has come about because some of the social costs of agglomeration are not fully borne by those who give rise to them in making their way in the world. To remedy this the collective sector should direct affairs so as to lead to a more socially rational configuration. This is the justification for land-use planning authority at the micro-scale and regional planning authority at the macro-geographic scope.

At the broader level, the assertion that our largest cities are beyond the optimal size does seem to find general acceptance. Policy-makers throughout the world have sought to disperse growth, especially to areas of high unemployment or low incomes with little urban development. In doing this it is recognized that a certain minimum concentration of activities is necessary for them to be economically viable. Thus we get 'growth poles' designated in peripheral regions of a nation.

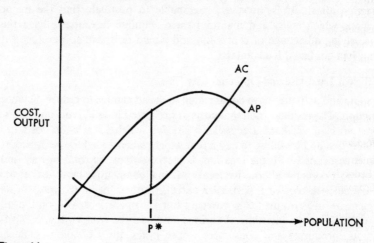

Figure 4.1

The argument for there being an optimum city size, which has somewhere been exceeded, depends on the notion of the average cost of urban facilities and production increasing beyond a certain population size, as congestion sets in. This is shown by the U-shaped curve (AC) in figure 4.1. We indulge in activities not merely to minimize their cost but to maximize the gap between cost and utility. In order for there to be a point of diminishing returns, it is necessary that the increase in average cost is accompanied by a decrease in productivity. This would be shown in a turn-down in the average product curve (AP) at some limiting population.

The optimum city size is then at that population where the difference between average cost and average product is at its greatest, as at P^* in figure 4.1. The argument that the largest of our towns are beyond this point depends on proof that the average product curve turns down at some point. There is no convincing evidence that this occurs at a population less than that of the largest cities.

The halting growth of major metropolitan areas on both sides of the Atlantic, coupled with a flight to the Sunbelt in the U.S.A. and a retrenchment of provincial identity in Britain, as the drift to the south ceases, is pointed to as evidence that the privately perceptible costs of agglomeration, never mind the external costs, have risen to intolerable levels. Such evidence is based on arbitrary, jurisdictional definitions of the urban area. Aided and abetted by market imperfections and local government fragmentation in the U.S.A. and by New-Town- and Green-Belt-style planning in the U.K., the urban agglomeration is taking on the far-flung, many-centred aspects of Los Angeles. Agglomeration is no longer tied to the single focus which fixed-rail, personal transport encouraged but takes on a more fluid, looser form, interspersed with open country and agricultural uses. This is largely a redistribution of a modestly growing or static population. Extension is fed from the decline of density about the old central focus. On this reading of circumstances it is hard to deny the continuing potency of the advantages of proximate location.

Readings

Internal economies of scale were analysed and quantified by J. S. Bain in 'Economies of scale, concentration and conditioning entry', *American Economic Review*, no. 44, 1954, pp. 15–39.

The geographical linkages and locational patterns of industry were described by S. P. Florence, in *Investment, Location and size of plant*, National Institute of Economic and Social Research, London, 1948.

A general source of these matters is R. C. Estall and R. O. Buchanan, *Industrial activity and economic geography*, Hutchinson, London, 1961.

The question of city size and efficiency is treated by W. Alonso in 'The economies of regional size', *Papers, Regional Science Association*, no. 26, 1971, pp. 67–83.

5. Trade and Travel

The Demand for Transport

It is a commonplace that the demand for transport is derived. Transport is not desired for its own sake: rather, its worth derives from the access it provides to other goods and services. The good 'transport' can for the most part be considered to have a negative utility. That is to say, its worth is negative, the less of it one has to consume the better. It is an irksome burden foisted upon us with the dimensions of direction and distance which we inhabit. People transport their goods and travel from place to place because they judge that it will afford them an excess of advantage over the cost in money, effort and irritation involved in the act of movement. The advantage does not arise from pushing a big rig down the M1 or from burning up the by-pass. The benefit accrues from the sale of your labour, the production and vending of goods, the consumption of goods and amenities or the enjoyment of meeting or entertainment. What motivates the demand for transport is a combination of the consumer's desire to maximize his well-being, coupled with the fact that production costs and, therefore, the free-on-board prices of goods vary between places. The issue is a little clouded by the tendency we have to turn necessity into a virtue and sugar the pill. The romance of rail and now the cult of trucking give transport the appearance of an end in itself. The fact is, however, that no matter how much glamour and fun we invest transport with, it remains a chore better avoided. Of course in our spare time we sometimes invert this negativity and seem to get a positive charge out of going for a spin or cruising. However, for the most part transport is of value insofar as it confers time and place utility on other goods, factors of production and service. It gets the goods to the right place at the right time.

This derivative nature of the demand for transport can be seen most clearly if we look at a simple example of trade in a good between two regions. Suppose the product is beef, which is produced and consumed in both regions 1 and 2. Without any trade between them, the prices in the two regions will be determined by local supply and demand conditions as in figure 5.1. Now, if there is a price difference as shown, this would provide a motive to buy beef in region 1 and ship and sell it in region 2, as long as

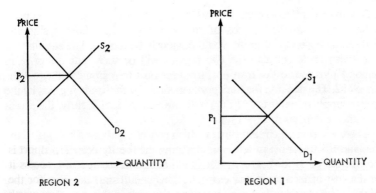

Figure 5.1

the price difference is greater than the cost of transport. A neat trick to show how this works involves swinging the quantity axis for region 2 around so that the supply and demand curves for the two regions are back to back. Then, to show the effect of transport costs on trade, the price axis of the exporting region, region 1, is shifted above that of the importing region by the cost of transporting one unit of the product from region 1 to region 2, as in figure 5.2. In this case, even with the cost of transport taken into account, a difference persists between the price in the two regions sufficient to make arbitrage profitable. One would expect trade to persist,

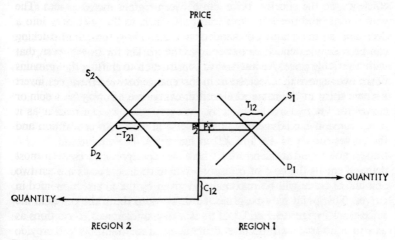

Figure 5.2

increasing the price in region 1 and lowering it in region 2 until the price difference just equalled the cost of transport. To persist in buying, shipping and selling beyond this point would obviously be foolish. The equilibrium price with trade between the two regions will be such that the price in region 1 plus the cost of transport from region 1 to region 2 will equal the price in 2. The demand for transport generated by this trade is given by the excess supply or exports of 1 (T_{12} in figure 5.2) or, equivalently, the excess demand or imports of 2 ($-T_{21}$).

There are several circumstances which can bring about a change in the demand for transport in terms of changing the locally determined prices. Production costs for beef may rise in either region because of an increase in the cost of feed-grain, for example. This would shift the supply curve in the affected region inwards, changing the price difference, the level of trade and, thus, the demand for transport. An increase in the level of employment in one region might cause an increase in the demand for beef at every price in that region and, thereby, the trade between regions. Relationships such as these underlie the correlation between trends in the general level of economic activity and the level of demand for transport. Unemployment decreases, real wages increase, demand for consumer goods and thus producer goods and raw materials increase at every possible price, thus trade increases and with it the demand for transport.

From figure 5.2 it should be clear that there is another factor which can affect the quantity of trade and that is the cost of transport. As the cost of transport decreases, due to investment in improved facilities or increased efficiency, so the effective price gap between regions increases and along with it trade and the volume of transport. Thus, as the price of transport decreases, so the quantity demanded increases. The graphic analysis above can be readily extended to incorporate the market for transport services with a variable price. An alternative construction to shifting the price axis of the two regions to reflect the transport change between them, consists of keeping them at the same level and drawing excess supply and demand curves for the two markets jointly. At every price we can read off how much demand exceeds supply or vice versa in each market and construct the curves shown as XS and XD in figure 5.3. The equilibrium level of trade is now found at the position where the gap between excess supply and demand equals the cost of transport. Where transport costs are zero the amount of trade will be maximal and given by the intersection of these curves. This point may be projected down onto the transport quantity/price graph in figure 5.3 at T^m. If transport charges exceed c^m on the price axis then no trade will occur and the demand for transport will be zero. The demand curve for transport may be constructed by joining these two points. If we can draw a supply curve for transport facilities, like ST in figure 5.3, then an equilibrium price for transport c^*, a quantity of transport demanded or of inter-regional trade T^* and prices for the good in the two regions P_1^* and P_2^* can be determined simultaneously.

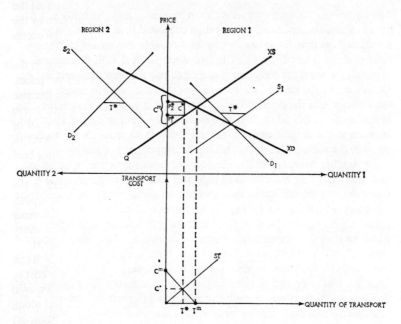

Figure 5.3

Having suggested that shippers respond to changes in the cost of transport and why, it behoves us to examine the shipper's perception of transport cost more closely. We have offered a motive for the demand curve for transport sloping down to the right and having a negative elasticity. The question we must ask now is: what is the price the shipper makes his decision with respect to? Is transport cost to the shipper just the rate charged times the tonnage or cube sent? It seems that shippers are increasingly conceiving of total distribution costs as the relevant item. The unit transport cost in figure 5.2, c_{12}, consists not only of the freight rate but must also take into account time and storage cost related elements. Simplified, the transport cost equation for a shipper would be:

$$\text{TRANSPORT COST} = rT + tT + sT$$

where $T = $ the quantity shipped in weight or bulk

   $r = $ the freight rate per weight or bulk per mile

   $t = $ in-transit costs, reflecting exposure to damage and pilferage

   $s = $ the cost of safety stock or inventory.

The latter item obviously varies with the frequency and reliability of transport in a more complicated fashion than suggested here. There is in general a trade-off so that the more regular and reliable the means of transport used and the lower the cost of buffer stock to deal with fluctuations in demand, the more the customer is willing to pay for such transport service. Details aside, the sum of all these elements is the value to match against the difference in the price at the factory or farm gate and that achievable in any market. In making a choice between different means of transport, between rail and road carriers, the shipper has to establish his trade-off between the various elements of his total transport costs equation.

To simplify matters further, suppose we can express the in-transit cost and safety stock items in terms of time and add them together. Clearly the faster delivery is, the lower the exposure to damage and the smaller the inventory which has to be kept. The shipper is involved in a trade-off between a cash price in the freight rate and a time price in the cost of having goods in transit and maintaining stock. The decision he makes between a slower, less reliable, cheaper form of transport, such as rail, and a faster, more reliable high-rate mode, such as road haulage, reveals the money value he places on speed, reliability and low inventory. The ratio of the difference in time taken by each mode to the difference in cash payments between the two yields a price for time. The same is true for personal travel. The choice between bus and train or car and bus can be viewed in the same fashion. Depending on how they value time, some people will choose more speed and less disposable income left, while those with a lower value on time will choose to keep more money for the same journey. The whole point of this discussion is that in marketing transport services or evaluating possible investments in transport facilities, the entrepreneur needs to know not only the sensitivity of demand with respect to the rate charged, but also with respect to the speed and reliability of the service.

These questions have been simplified for exposition. Time as such, or speed, might or might not be important. It obviously is with perishable goods such as liquid milk or cut flowers. It certainly is for people travelling to work or for travelling salesmen. In some cases time as such is a handy proxy measure for exposure to damage and thieving. However, for shippers of large quantities in a regular flow, for whom a transport leg is part of the production line, time is not so important. They can programme in a transport element to their processing arrangements of whatever speed a carrier can achieve, as long as the carrier's rate of delivery is reliable. Indeed, it may be advantageous to leave part of their buffer stock in the pipeline rather than in costly warehouse space.

In discussing the demand for transport there is cause for caution before drawing a traditional demand curve between quantity and price axes. We have suggested that the price shippers perceive is a somewhat complex matter. The fact is that quantity is, too. We are dealing with the most heterogeneous of goods, apart from real estate. What the customer is buying is capacity to carry particular goods between specific places at specific times, not a lump of 'transport'.

The demand for transport is also complicated because the choices which shippers have to make in the long run involve interdependencies between the kind and amount of transport to be used, the location of factories, the input mix to be used in production, the product mix to be used in output, and the markets to be penetrated. For the theory we are considering in this chapter these are the *ceteris* which are *paribus*. Location was the variable of analysis in Chapter 2. Despite this distinction, we must recognize here that fundamental transport demand decisions are made when a plant is located and its production process and markets are established. One of the premier considerations in siting is the minimization of the costs of access to raw materials and factors of production, including labour, and to markets. The decision where to build may select a mode of transport by choosing a site accessible by rail, road or waterway. The production batch size and loading facility investment made at the outset may lock a factory into a particular transport medium. Given the prevalence of such circumstances, there is obviously a massive stability about market shares between different means of transport. Of the total quantity of freight moving in the U.S.A., less than 25 per cent is actively competed for between transport modes. In the U.K. the figure is down in the 10 per cent range. For the most part the division of freight between road, rail and water carriers does seem insensitive to small price changes.

In the intermodally competitive portion of the market, short-run decisions on the kind and quantity of transport to purchase are closely interwoven with decisions on the timing of sales and purchases. Cattle dealers might be willing to pay highly for rapid road shipment if they expect a downturn in meat prices in the near future. In Britain, the Ford Motor Company used to purchase components for its cars on a very short order basis to avoid contractual ties and enjoy the advantages of shopping around. The lack of regularity in the pattern of sources made the transport cost of assembling these materials high, but that was obviously overwhelmed by the purchase price advantage. The lack of regularity and short-term basis of the operation made it vulnerable to disruption and costly crisis solutions. In the extreme a plane would be chartered to fly in a bag of bolts, for the opportunity cost of such high transport expenditure was that of stopping a car assembly line, beside which it dwindled to insignificance.

What emerges from all this is that when we specify the demand for transport we really have to get down to details. It is also the case that the relevant quantitative specification of demand varies with the purpose of analysis. We can distinguish a hierarchy of levels of demand for transport with each level of aggregation suited to different types of investment or marketing decision.

At the most aggregate level there is the total quantity of transport which occurs in the nation in any time interval, expressed in tons or ton-mile equivalents. This is not particularly useful to anyone, though it might provide an index for some rough budgetary allocation exercise at the Treasury level. The quantity of all transport for some categories of means of transport is possibly more useful. For example, it might be desired to evaluate some policy proposals for reducing energy consumption in the transport sector by promoting technological and operational improvements. To get the order of magnitude estimates of the likely savings, which are all that one could aspire to in such an endeavour, it would be necessary to project current figures of total ton miles by major transport media, under assumptions of no great change, as a do-nothing baseline against which to evaluate the methods and policies proposed.

When the quantity of transport acquires a commodity label, be it for one or all modes, then it becomes relevant to the industrial sector. The total number of passenger miles is a relevant figure for fleet-capacity decisions by large carriers. The total volume of coal being carried is an important datum for those who manufacture coal wagons.

A geographical index on the quantity of a good transported by a particular mode, indicating where it originates or terminates, may be relevant to the planning of terminal facilities. In the mid-60s, the Ministry of Transport made estimates of the quantities of goods which would flow through various ports in order to determine how much and where container port capacity should be permitted or fostered.

What the customer usually wants is to move a certain quantity of a good or himself from one place to another. This origin-destination flow is the most pertinent notion of the quantity of transport. However, when we consider the operation of the means of transport, a more detailed specification yet is needed. The operator needs to have information about quantities travelling over particular routes so as to manage capacity and schedule services. In the case of personal travel by car, the customers are the operators and they have to make routing decisions themselves. We will turn to the problems which this coincidence generates when we look at the pricing of transport services and the supply of transport infrastructure.

Travel and Social Physics

Faced with a somewhat heterogeneous class of traffic to explain, such as parcels or, especially, passengers, it is straining belief to formulate demand in the deterministic fashion we have employed so far. The theory of trade employed at the outset of this chapter prohibits cross-hauling in its solution. Passenger travel, parcels and mail obviously do not obey such rules. When contemplating a single, homogeneous commodity, it is reasonable to postulate a simple objective motivating the demand for transport, such as satisfying demand by supply with a minimum transport cost. It is not reasonable to characterize the myriad of motives for personal travel or a traffic volume representing the flow of a whole spectrum of goods so simply. Given a lack of knowledge and uncertainty about the processes involved, the inclination is to turn from the deterministic to the probabilistic. Whether one is drawn philosophically towards Heisenberg's elevation of uncertainty to the status of a principle or, with Laplace, regards chance as an ultimately remediable shortcoming of the human condition, one can incorporate uncertainty into a theory by representing a chancy process by a suitable probability function. This has been the main resort in trying to predict personal travel and more aggregate demands for transport services.

Since the triumph of Newtonian physics many investigators of the behaviour of man have attempted to emulate the physical sciences by using their methods and going to their theories for analogies. Of particular interest to geographers has been the use of 'gravity models' to describe the movement of people and goods and the strength of communication between communities, and the use of 'potential models' to explore the advantages of people in various locations from the point of view of interacting with others. Indeed, Newton's rival Leibniz is credited with first proposing that social phenomena could be analysed in terms of time and space.

Very generally, the gravity model says that the interaction, I_{ij}, between any two communities i and j is directly proportional to the product of the masses of the two, M_i and M_j, and inversely proportional to some function of the distance between them, d_{ij}. This can be converted into an equation by the insertion of a constant of proportionality, k.

So we have:

$$I_{ij} = \frac{k.M.M_j}{f(d_{ij})}.$$

The masses can be expressed in terms of either population or population weighted by some relevant characteristic such as income. The function of distance will represent the mapping into geographical space of social or economic distance.

The potential for interaction of an individual in area i with the populations in all other areas, j, in the universe under consideration, is given by:

$$V_i = k \sum_j \frac{M_j}{d_{ij}}.$$

Gravity models have attracted a growing amount of attention over the last twenty years by dint of their use in traffic and land-use planning. Their strategic role in the policy-making process made it important that their shaky theoretical foundation – and hence many loose ends in operation – be consolidated. A major contribution to this effort was made by Wilson (1967). He derived a tightened-up version of the gravity model, using an elegant and quite general model building method from statistical mechanics.

Given uncertainty about the behaviour of people in travelling between various locations, the probability of an overall pattern of trips is assumed to be given by a probability function, the binomial distribution. From this it is possible to determine the particular arrangement of all the possible trips which is associated with the maximum value of the function, subject to certain constraints representing what is known to be true about the system. This will constitute the 'most probable' state of this system. In the case of travel between places where we know the number of trips which start and finish in each place, the most likely configuration turned out to be given by an expression akin to the gravity equation:

$$T_{ij} = \frac{A_i B_j O_i D_j}{e^{\beta cij}}$$

such that:

$$A_i = \frac{1}{\sum_j B_j D_j / e^{\beta cij}}$$

$$B_j = \frac{1}{\sum A_i D_i / e^{\beta cij}}$$

Where T_{ij} = the flow of people from origin i to destination j
O_i = the total number of trips starting from origin i
D_j = the total number of trips ending in destination j
c_{ij} = the cost of travel from origin i to destination j
β = a coefficient describing the sensitivity of the volume of travel to cost

and A_i and B_j are balancing factors which ensure that no more trips are predicted to start in i than O_i and end in j than D_j.

The fashion in which this end-point is reached from the relatively innocuous-looking assumptions with which we started, is detailed in Appendix I to this chapter.

Pricing Transport Services

Earlier in this chapter the explanation of transport sector prices given was by way of a description of how markets operate so as to balance demands and supplies. Whether the equilibrium achieved in this fashion is satisfactory from a social point of view is not clear. We now need to put the normative question: what is the right price, and thus quantity used, for a good or service in terms of meeting the needs of the whole of society?

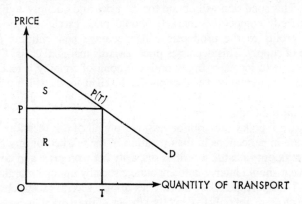

Figure 5.4

Suppose that the demand for road haulage between two towns can be described by a downward-sloping demand curve such as $P(T)$ in figure 5.4. We want now to find values for price P and quantity of transport T which will produce the greatest well-being for society, i.e. maximize social welfare. Welfare may be defined as the difference between the benefits which an activity generates for everyone and the cost it imposes on everyone. Let us assume that transport generates no costs to anyone but the carrier. In addition, we assume that benefit is captured in what the shipper receives as revenue and the difference between what the shippers would have been willing to pay and what they actually paid. This surplus accruing to consumers is measurable as the area under the demand curve above the price paid, S in figure 5.4. With these assumptions we can write the equation for social welfare as follows:

$$\text{WELFARE} = \text{SOCIAL BENEFITS} - \text{SOCIAL COSTS}$$
$$= \text{REVENUE} + \text{CONSUMER SURPLUS} -$$
$$\text{TOTAL COST}$$

Clearly, the consumer surplus element S will be larger the lower the price. The other part of the welfare expression has to be satisfied by covering costs of providing the transport service from the revenue. The lowest price which will ensure costs are covered is one which equals the additional cost resulting from increasing the quantity of transport provided by one unit. According to this theory therefore, the well-being of society is maximized by setting the price of transport, or indeed of any good, equal to the cost of producing the last unit sold, i.e. the marginal cost. A brief mathematical treatment of this point is given in Appendix II of this chapter. This condition will obtain for the price and quantity equilibrium of a perfectly competitive market. Should price exceed marginal cost, surplus profits to the producers will encourage new entrants and an increase of supply. This depresses price towards marginal costs. Entrants will continue to increase supply until the point of equality is reached. A price below marginal cost will imply dead-weight losses which will drive producers out of business, thereby reducing supply and pushing price up towards the same equilibrium.

The general policy prescription arising from all of this therefore is that, if there are imperfections in the operation of the market for any good or service sufficient to cause a serious disparity between price and costs, the government should intervene to encourage socially optimal marginal cost pricing. Transport facilities and services display several salient characteristics which seem not only to deny the efficacy of the market in determining the quantity supplied, but also the value of the simple marginal-cost pricing rule.

In the first place, the long gestation period and sheer magnitude of investment requirements for the travelling way and terminals of transport systems have often put them beyond the scope of unsupported commercial interest. In addition, the political indispensability of good communications in terms of military and administrative access in forming or maintaining territorial hegemony supersedes all other considerations. There is also an ingrained, traditional, popular view of some transport facilities as a 'public good' which should be provided and paid for collectively. This is especially true for roads. This attitude is not without a sensible basis. Up to the present, and for some time to come, the cost of operating a place-and time-specific price mechanism and excluding non-payers throughout the road network, would greatly exceed the additional well-being resulting from a more precise equation of individual use of roads and the costs arising.

Even if we put these political and practical matters aside and consider the classical, natural monopoly case for intervention, marginal-cost pricing still presents difficulties. The natural monopoly argument was used to justify the control government exercised over railways in the last century and it clings as regulatory entanglement long after their monopoly was broken by road motor vehicles. The argument for control asserts that some forms of transport, such as railways, because of their enormous initial capital costs and relatively small unit cost of running, enjoy continually decreasing costs over the entire market. Thus they constitute natural monopolies which can readily exclude new entrants and control either supply or price so as to extract excess profits from their customers. Thus they require strict government control of their prices and conditions of service to ensure that this power is not abused at the expense of national efficiency.

In attempting to apply the marginal-cost pricing prescription, three difficulties arise.

Firstly, if average cost decreases as output increases, then the cost of producing the last unit of output must always be below cost averaged over all units of output. Total costs are the product of this average cost and quantity output. Clearly, the revenue generated by charging marginal-cost prices will never cover total costs.

Secondly, the extensive and costly networks of transport ways seriously strain the concept of costs in which the theory is phrased. Additions to a network to meet increasing requirements for movement tend to be made in big chunks, such as new lengths of road or track. When the service capacity of the existing system is saturated, the next unit of output requires an enormous and dramatic addition. Whether one can sensibly talk of marginal cost in such circumstances is questionable.

Finally, there is an argument, and indeed a theorem, which says that if prices tend to exceed marginal costs in much of the rest of the economy, then to enforce marginal-cost prices in one sector will not necessarily improve welfare.

The difficulties we have raised are of most concern in advanced economies where transport policy issues concern substitution between a stagnant or declining rail industry and a growing road-haulage industry. In such a case the prices have to be right at the competitive margin to prevent a misallocation of resources. In developing areas, the transport sector as a whole is insufficient for needs and the policy issue is how to add any kind of transport capacity to assist the expansion of the rest of the economy. The big question is how to recover the total cost of additions to capacity. If the country in question intends to rely on roads to meet its needs, as most will, the problem is not so acute. Road costs which change in proportion to the volume of transport carried may be recovered by the government with a fuel tax incident on road users. If the total cost of providing roads exceeds the sum of these marginal costs, the remainder may be recovered legitimately by taxing those whose land's value is enhanced by the accessibility which roads afford. We shall see later that the benefit of improved transport is ultimately reflected in the value of land. The U.S. Government was responsible for the most ingenious example of this method of recovering the development costs of providing transport services. To finance the extension of the railway network west of the Mississippi, the Congress gave the railroads half of the land within the range where the proposed line was likely to encourage commercial agriculture. This was sold to defray the costs of construction. Then the price the government asked for the other half was doubled. So encouragement to railroads cost the government nothing in cash terms. Although historical circumstances are unlikely to afford the chance of detailed imitation of this scheme, nevertheless the principle of recovering construction costs by charges on improved property values is generally applicable.

Measurement of Transport Benefits

No matter how the cost of construction and operation of a road or piece of track is recovered, there remains the problem of measuring the benefits it will generate in order to judge whether they exceed this cost. There is no point in building or promoting new capacity if its benefits do not exceed costs. The social benefit of a good was previously defined as the consumer surplus plus producer surplus or total revenue, i.e. the area $S+R$ in figure 5.4. Road space in particular is a non-marketable, essentially collective good. There is no market price which registers what the use of a piece of road is worth to the marginal customer. There are no observations on price and quantity demanded from which to estimate the shape of a demand curve. Despite the absence of a market, road and public transport users do vary their use in response to a 'price'. The price paid includes expenditure of the traveller's time, including that spent in walking to and from parked vehicles. When we consider public transport, waiting time is obviously relevant. The price also has a cash component including tolls, parking charges, fares and vehicle running costs. This combination of time and money outlays is referred to as the 'generalized cost' of travel. In making choices between means of travel or routes or indeed whether to travel at all, the consumer behaves according to his perception of these costs. Observations of users' choices between routes and modes with different time and cash costs will reveal the value placed on time and how that varies between different uses of time. In Great Britain it has been found that in general people value non-working time spent in a vehicle travelling at about 40 per cent of their wage rate, while time spent walking and waiting is twice as costly. If we wish to predict demand or choices then clearly these behavioural costs are the appropriate explanatory variable.

However, economic evaluation of a policy or investment is concerned with estimating the real resources consumed in travel and transport. The resources used up in travel may vary from those perceived by the consumer in two ways. The prices that people face may not reflect the resource cost of travel. For example, in the price paid for fuel there is an element of taxation not representing a resource cost. Frequently the fare charged on public transport may not reflect the cost of operation, either in total or in part. In addition, people's knowledge and perception are imperfect. There is evidence which suggests that the average estimate of the cost of running a car is somewhat less than a precise engineering assessment of the marginal mileage cost. These departures should obviously be adjusted to in making decisions on the allocation of resources.

If we leave these niceties aside and assume perfect knowledge and marginal-cost prices, then the benefit of a transport improvement can be quite simply measured. An investment is undertaken to reduce the generalized cost of travel. If travel is a normal good this should result in an increase in demand. We can observe the generalized cost and demand for travel before the improvement, C_1 and T_1 in figure 5.5. If we can predict these values after the improvement is in place, C_2 and T_2, then we can measure the change in consumer surplus over doing nothing to compare with the cost. If we assume that the demand curve is linear over the relevant range, then the increment in consumer surplus, the shaded area in figure 5.5, is given quite simply by:

$$\Delta CS = \tfrac{1}{2} (T_1 + T_2) (C_1 - C_2).$$

This chapter started by remarking the derivative nature of the demand for transport. Then surely it can be objected that the benefits of transport

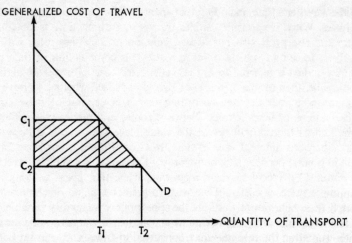

Figure 5.5

improvements will ultimately accrue in the markets for final goods and not merely in the market for the means of their carriage. However, in a perfectly competitive economy the effects of a transport improvement in all the markets for final goods, measured by consumer surplus and profits, is equalled and represented by the change in consumer surplus in the transport market. This then provides an adequate measure of the entire increase in well-being to the economy. Proof of this is given in Appendix III.

Appendix I

**Wilson's Derivation of a Gravity Model
for Distributing Trips Between Zones in a Town.**

(After the original in A. G. Wilson, 'A statistical theory of spatial distribution models', *Transportation Research*, no. 1, 1967, pp. 253–69.)

Suppose we have an urban area divided into a system of zones which are both origins and destinations between which people make trips, say, places of residence and work. As origins we label them i and as destinations j. There is a given total number of trips in the urban area, T, and we know the number of trips that will be generated at each origin, O_i, and attracted by each destination, D_j. We also know the cost of moving between each pair of zones, c_{ij}. For simplicity's sake, we assume that no trips cross the town's boundary in either direction, so

$$T = \sum_i O_i = \sum_j D_j.$$

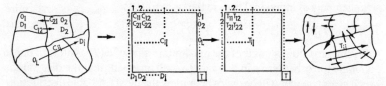

Figure 5.6

In figure 5.6 we see how a map of the town is transformed into a matrix with rows as origins and columns as destinations and the cost of moving between any pair of zones as the elements. The problem is to produce a general mathematical expression for a distribution of T, a set of flows between is and js. designated T_{ij}. In the figure, this is shown as an origin destination matrix of flows of people, which can then be mapped as a 'desire-line' pattern. The mathematical expression must produce estimates of T_{ij} so as to satisfy three constraints representing ways in which we know the system does behave:

$$\sum_j T_{ij} = O_i, \text{ a constraint on availabilities;} \qquad \ldots 1$$

$\sum\limits_{i} T_{ij} = D_j$, a constraint on requirements; ...2

and $\sum\limits_{i} \sum\limits_{j} T_{ij}.c_{ij} = C$, which says that the total amount ...3

spent on travel in the town is a fixed amount C.

Now the number of distinct arrangements of individual trips which accord with a particular configuration of bundles of trips, T_{ij}, is the number of ways T_{11} can be selected from T, T_{12} from $T-T_{11}$, T_{13} from $T-T_{11}-T_{12}$ etc., which we designated $\omega(T_{ij})$. This is given by the binomial expansion:

$$\omega(T_{ij})$$

$$= \frac{T!}{T_{11}!(T-T_{11})!} \cdot \frac{(T-T_{11})!}{T_{12}!(T-T_{11}-T_{12})!} \cdot \frac{(T-T_{11}-T_{12})!}{T_{13}!(T-T_{11}-T_{12}-T_{13})!} \ \cdots$$

so cancelling through the $(T-T_{ij})!$ terms we get:

$$\omega(T_{ij}) = \frac{T!}{\prod\limits_{ij} T_{ij}!}$$

where $\prod$ indicates the multiplication of the T_{ij} terms.

If we sum these $\omega(T_{ij})$ values over all the distributions which satisfy constraints (1), (2) and (3) we obtain the total number of possible distinct arrangements of individual trips in the system (W):

$$W = \Sigma\omega(T_{ij}).$$

Wilson next points out that the maximum value of $\omega(T_{ij})$ will turn out to dominate the other terms in this sum to such an extent that the distribution which gives rise to it will be overwhelmingly the most probable distribution.

The argument is difficult to follow in the abstract, so a simple two-by-two example may prove useful at this stage. Consider two areas with four trips, to be distributed between them without any constraints. In figure 5.7 we can enumerate all the possible T_{ij} and calculate values for $\omega(T_{ij})$. The T_{ij} which coincides with the maximum value is the most probable – it coincides with the largest number of possible individual arrangements. In the unconstrained case (a), the uniform distribution, coinciding with 24 possible distinct arrangements of individual trips, is the most probable. We can now introduce constraints on availabilities and requirements. Let $T = 10$ and $O_1 = 4$, $O_2 = 6$, $D_1 = 5$ and $D_2 = 5$. We can enumerate the T_{ij} which satisfy these constraints and evaluate $\omega(T_{ij})$. In this case (c), the most uniform distribution which satisfies the constraints is the most

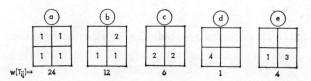

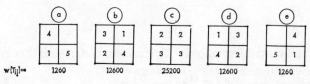

Figure 5.7

probable. The reader will see that in each case a change in one part from the most probable T_{ij} leads to a halving of the value of $\omega(T_{ij})$.

Coming back to our general statement, we wish to find an expression for a set of T_{ij} which will maximize $\omega(T_{ij})$ subject to (1), (2) and (3). To obtain such an expression we maximize the following:

$$M = \log \omega + \sum_i \lambda_i \, (O_i - \sum_j T_{ij}) + \sum_j \lambda_j \, (D_j - \sum_i T_{ij}) + \beta(C - \sum_i \sum_j T_{ij}.c_{ij})$$

where λ_i, λ_j and β are Lagrangean multipliers. The log of $\omega(T_{ij})$ has been taken to facilitate the use of Stirling's approximation to estimate the

factorial terms in $\dfrac{T!}{\prod\limits_{ij} T_{ij}!}$. Any monotonic function of ω will give rise to the

same answer. To maximize the function we equate its partial derivative with respect to T_{ij} to zero:

$$\frac{\partial M}{\partial T_{ij}} = 0.$$

Now Stirling's approximation gives: $\dfrac{\partial \log N!}{\partial N} = \log N$, and so

$$\frac{\partial M}{\partial T_{ij}} = -\log T_{ij} - \lambda_i - \lambda_j - \beta \ c_{ij}$$

and this expression becomes zero when

$$T_{ij} = e^{-\lambda_i - \lambda_j - \beta c_{ij}}.$$

This can be demonstrated by substituting for T_{ij} in the derivative:

$$\frac{\partial M}{\partial T_{ij}} = -\log |e^{-\lambda_i - \lambda_j - \beta c_{ij}}| - \lambda_i - \lambda_j - \beta c_{ij}.$$

Now $\log e^x = x$.

Therefore $\dfrac{\partial M}{\partial T_{ij}} = - | -\lambda_i - \lambda_j - \beta c_{ij} | -\lambda_i - \lambda_j - \beta c_{ij}$

so $\dfrac{\partial M}{\partial T_{ij}} = 0$.

If we substitute this solution for T_{ij} into constraints (1) and (2) we get:

$$e^{-\lambda i} = \frac{O_i}{\sum_j e^{-\lambda_j - \beta c_{ij}}}, \text{ and } e^{-\lambda j} = \frac{D_j}{\sum_i e^{-\lambda_i - \beta c_{ij}}}.$$

To simplify the notation we can let

$$\frac{e^{-\lambda_i}}{O_i} = A_i, \text{ and } \frac{e^{-\lambda_i}}{D_j} = B_j$$

so that

$$T_{ij} = A_i.B_j.O_i.D_j.e^{-\beta c_{ij}}$$

where

$$A_i = |\sum_j B_j.D_j.e^{-\beta c_{ij}}|^{-1} \text{ and } B_j = |\sum A_i.O_i.e^{-\beta c_{ij}}|^{-1}.$$

This is known as the 'doubly constrained gravity model'. That this formulation satisfies the constraints can be shown by substituting it for T_{ij} in each constraint:

(1) $\sum_j T_{ij} = O_i$

$$\sum_j (A_i.B_j.O_i.D_j.e^{-\beta cij}) = O_i.$$

Since we are summing over j there are only single values of A_i and O_i, so we can rearrange this to give:

$$A_i = |\sum B_j.D_j.e^{-\beta c_{ij}}|^{-1}$$

and similarly for B_j.

So Wilson's derivation shows that the most probable distribution of trips is given by a gravity model. C in constraint (3) need not be known, and in practice β is estimated from empirical data in trip-making behaviour, although if C were known a numerical value of β could be solved for.

It is perhaps worthwhile, at this juncture, saying a few words about the application of this model for prediction. A future set of O_i's and D_j's and c_{ij}'s is given. As has been suggested, β is estimated from empirical data on current behaviour using a curve-fitting technique, such as least squares. To obtain values for A_i and B_j, all B_j's are set to some arbitrary value, say one. These are then inserted in the equation for A_i. The set of values of A_i calculated are inserted in the equation for B_j and a new set of B_j's calculated. This 'iterative' procedure is continued until the values of the two sets of factors converge to stability. Then estimates of T_{ij} can be made.

The function which describes the rate at which the number of trips falls off with increasing cost in this formulation comes out as an exponential, $e^{-\beta c_{ij}}$. This does not agree in many cases with empirically fitted forms, especially when we examine inter-urban and long-distance interaction. In such cases a Pareto function of the form $d_{ij}^{-\beta}$ replicates the real pattern better. However, Wilson's derivation is in terms of cost of movement, whereas most inter-urban empirical work has had to be satisfied with distance as a proxy for cost. We can postulate that for long journeys cost will vary as the log of distance. We know that the marginal cost of distance decreases as the length of trip increases, largely because of the spreading of overhead costs which must be incurred no matter what distance is travelled over great mileage. If we replace c_{ij} in the total cost constraint above by $\log d_{ij}$ to give:

$$\sum_i \sum_j T_{ij} . \log d_{ij} = C$$

and go through the algebra again, we do in fact end up with a gravity model of the form:

$$T_{ij} = A_i . B_j . O_i . D_j . d_{ij}^{-\beta}.$$

Apart from presenting a theoretical justification for the gravity model, Wilson's approach offers a quite general principle for model building. The only theoretical assumption made is that the probability of a distribution is proportional to the number of distinct individual arrangements possible in the system subject to a number of constraints. To build a model in this manner we designate a set of variables which define the system, express hypotheses by writing down constraints on these variables to restrict their behaviour in ways it is known are not random, and then obtain an expression which maximizes the probability subject to the constraints. The log of ω which is maximized in the above derivation is defined in statistical mechanics as 'entropy' and this is equivalent to the definition of entropy in information theory. The approach is thus called the 'entropy maximizing' method of model building.

Appendix II

Welfare Maximizing Prices

In the text welfare was expressed as the sum of total revenue and consumer surplus less total costs; we can write this:

$$W = R + S - C.$$

To maximize welfare, this expression is differentiated with respect to quantity (T) and the derivatives set equal to zero:

$$\frac{\partial W}{\partial T} = \frac{d(R+S)}{dT} - \frac{dC}{dT} = 0.$$

Now the rate at which revenue plus consumer surplus change as quantity changes is price because:

$$R + S = \int_0^T p(T)\, dT$$

so

$$\frac{d(R+S)}{dT} = \frac{d}{dT} \int_0^T p(T)\, dT = p(T),\ \text{since the differentiation of an integral}$$

with respect to its argument yields the original function. The derivative of total cost with respect to quantity is marginal cost:

$$\frac{dC}{pT} = M.C.$$

Thus, in order to maximize welfare:

$$W\,MAX = p - MC = 0$$
$$p = MC$$

prices must be set equal to marginal cost.

Appendix III

Holtermann's Demonstration of the Equality of Transport Benefits and Final Market Benefits

(After the original in A. J. Harrison and S. E. Holtermann, 'Economic appraisal of transport projects and urban planning objectives', mimeo, Centre for Environmental Studies, London, June 1973.)

It is required to prove that the change in consumer surplus in the transport market, due to a reduction in the price of transport, is equal to all the changes in profits and consumer surplus in the markets for final goods which are influenced. This requirement may be written:

$$\Delta\, CS \text{ TRANSPORT} = \Delta\, CS \text{ FINAL GOODS} +$$
$$\Delta \text{ PROFIT FINAL GOODS} + \Delta \text{ PROFIT OTHER FACTORS}$$

The prices of final goods and of other factors used in the production of final goods are allowed to change in response to the fall in the price of transport. The diagram, figure 5.8, shows final demand and supply in the transport, final good and factor markets after all prices have adjusted.

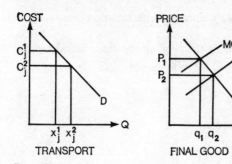
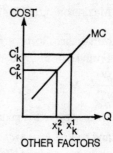

Figure 5.8

As transport costs fall from c_j^1 to c_j^2, the marginal cost of producing final good q falls and, given perfect competition, results in a fall in its price from p_1 to p_2. The demand for other factors of production falls or rises, as do their costs. To simplify matters it is assumed that all factors except k are produced under constant returns to scale, so that their prices and profits do not change.

The first two quantities we wish to assess are:
transport consumer surplus

$$\Delta CS_j = - \int x_j\, dc_j$$

and final good consumer surplus

$$\Delta CS_q = -\int q\, dp:$$

We also have to assess profit changes resulting from the transport price change. To do this we assume that the entire demand for factors of production derives from the production of the final good, i.e. that transport is not used in the production of factor k and vice versa.

The demand for final good $q = F(p)$. Its production function is $q = f(x_1, \ldots, x_i, \ldots x_n)$ and profits are given by:

$$\Pi_q = p\, f(x_1 \ldots, x_n) - \Sigma\, c_i\, x_i$$

the difference between revenue and costs. The first order conditions for the maximization of this profit function are:

$$p f_i = c_i\ (i = 1 \ldots n). \qquad\qquad 1$$

This states that the ratio of the prices of goods be equal to the ratio of their marginal products. For factor k, the production function is

$$x_k = g(x_1 \ldots, x_i, \ldots x_n),\ (i \neq j,\ i \neq k).$$

Maximizing profit for factor k yields first order conditions:

$$c_k g_i = c_i\ (i = 1 \ldots n,\ i \neq j,\ i \neq k). \qquad\qquad 2$$

From all of this, equilibrium levels of x_i, q and p, and c_k emerge as functions of c_j, in particular c_k is a function of c_j, so that

$$d c_k = \frac{\partial c_k}{\partial c_j}\, dc_j$$

and p is a function of c_j, so that

$$d p = \frac{\partial p}{\partial c_j}\, dc_j.$$

We are now in a position to express all the surplus and profit changes as a function of the changes in transport costs:

$$\Delta CS_q = -\int q\,dp = \int q\frac{\partial p}{\partial c_j}\,dc_j$$

and $\Delta\Pi p = \int \dfrac{\partial \Pi q}{\partial c_j}\,dc_j$

$$= \int \left\{ \frac{\partial p}{\partial c_j}q + p\sum_i f_i\frac{\partial x_i}{\partial c_j} - \sum_i c_i\frac{\partial x_i}{\partial c_j} - x_j - x_k\frac{\partial c_k}{\partial c_j} \right\}dc_j.$$

By substitution from (1) this becomes:

$$= \int \left\{ \frac{\partial p}{\partial c_j}q - x_j - x_k\frac{\partial c_k}{\partial c_j} \right\}dc_j$$

Finally, the profit from factors of production:

$$\Delta\Pi_k = \int \frac{\partial \Pi_k}{\partial c_j}\,dc_j$$

and by substitution from (2) this becomes:

$$= \int \left\{ x_k\frac{\partial c_k}{\partial c_j} + c_k\sum_{\substack{i\neq j \\ i\neq \cdot}} g_i\frac{\partial x_i}{\partial c_j} - \sum_{\substack{i\neq j \\ i\neq k}} c_i\frac{\partial x_i}{\partial c_j} \right\}dc_j$$

so $\Delta CSq + \Delta\Pi q + \Delta\Pi k =$

$$-\int q\frac{\partial p}{\partial c_j}dc_j + \int \left\{ \frac{\partial p}{\partial c_j}q - x_j - x_k\frac{\partial c_k}{\partial c_j} \right\}dc_j + \int \left\{ x_k\frac{\partial c_k}{\partial c_j} + c_k\sum_{\substack{i\neq j \\ i\neq k}} g_i\frac{\partial x_i}{\partial c_j} \right.$$

$$\left. - \sum_{\substack{i\neq j \\ i\neq k}} c_i\frac{\partial x_i}{\partial c_j} \right\}dc_j,$$ and this expression cancels term by term leaving:

$-\int x_j\,dc_j$ which is the change in consumer surplus in the transport market. Thus the value of this quantity in the transport market equals and represents all the changes in final goods and product markets.

Readings

P. A. Samuelson presents a theory of price geography and trade in 'Spatial price equilibrium and linear programming', *American Economic Review*, no. 42, 1952, pp. 283–303. A collection of papers on the demand for transport has been edited by R. E. Quandt, *The demand for travel: theory and measurement*, Heath Lexington, Lexington, Massachusetts, 1970. This includes A. G. Wilson's gravity model derivation. Wilson presents a more complete picture of the application of statistical methods to predicting geographical behaviour in *Entropy in urban and regional planning*, Pion, London, 1970.

The economics of freight transport, in the U.S.A. at least, is treated in J. R. Meyer, M. J. Peck, J. Stenason and C. Zwick, *The economics of competition in the transportation industries*, Harvard University Press, Cambridge, Massachusetts, 1959.

The transport of people in cities is covered by J. R. Meyer, J. F. Kain, and M. Wohl, *The urban transportation problem*, Harvard University Press, Cambridge, Massachusetts, 1968.

The measurement of the social benefits of transport is dealt with by A. J. Harrison in *The economics of transport appraisal*, Croom Helm, London, 1975.

6. Transport Facilities

Expansion of a Transport Network

The very fact of being centrally located is in itself an advantage in terms of overcoming the friction of distance. In most regions of the world this advantage is accentuated by a transport network structure which focuses accessibility even more powerfully on the centre.

This effect is best illustrated with a simple abstraction. Suppose we start with a farming society, subsisting in a circular, evenly fertile plain, on which travel is equally costly in all directions. All travel is in straight lines between origins and destinations. There is no transport network. Let there be some slight degree of specialization of production and trade, so that every small area produces some product which is sold to farmers all over the plain. Even if the amounts to be transported per unit area are everywhere the same, the cost of trading will vary over the plain. The point of minimum aggregated travel is at the centre and transport costs decrease from there outwards. Consider a diameter of the circular plain and take every point along it, calculating the sum of the distances from that point to every other point. It seems obvious that this value, the travel cost of our example, will be largest at the ends of the line and smallest at the centre. If we draw a line as in figure 6.1, consisting of five points separated by

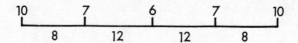

Figure 6.1

intervals one mile long, then the sum of distances from each point to every other are the numbers above the line. If we rotate this through 360° about an axis at the centre then we will describe a set of contours of travel cost representing a bowl-like surface, lowest at the centre and highest at the edge as in figure 6.2a. Such a difference in transport cost would in itself be an inducement for a movement of labour and rearrangement of activities. The production of goods which could bid the highest for use of land because of the higher prices they command and/or the high transport costs they incur because of great bulk, weight or perishability, would gravitate towards the centre of the plain and occupy it more densely. Let us for the present leave such tendencies aside and assume that the density remains uniform and the location of tradeable surpluses of various goods is a response to slight local variations in soil type, climate or tradition.

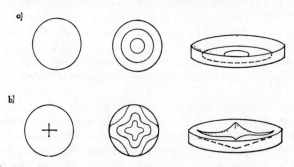

Figure 6.2

Suppose now that the effort of traversing mired tracks to trade is irritating and perceived to be costly and that the technology of road building and its advantages are known. Roadway is very costly to construct. Its bed at least, and certainly its right of way, has a life of generations. It requires governmental authority over the use of land to coordinate its alignment. Finally, it is exceptionally costly to recover the cost of providing it by pricing which involves exclusion of non-payers. It is in short a collective good, best provided by public enterprise. If the farmers in our plain are under some kind of social contract, then an authority with the brief to employ some of the surplus gathered for governmental uses as tax can invest it to build roads. Imagine that at the outset the annual budget for roads is only enough to build one mile of road. Supposing some kind of popular basis for government, we can assume that the road authority's constitution mandates it to reduce total transport costs as much as possible with the available resources. Building roads reduces transport costs by increasing the speed and reducing the resources needed to carry goods and people. This leaves more time and wealth for leisure or production. More speed means moving the same amount of trade with, say, fewer draught animals. This reduces the need for fodder and releases land for other uses. On the other hand the same resources could be used to carry more trade. Given its mandate, in seeking a site for the first mile of road, the authority will seek the location where traffic density is greatest. By putting the road capacity in there it can reduce the transport bill of society by the greatest amount. This will again be at the centre of its plain, with an arbitrary selection of direction. If we look at a diameter of the plain abstracted to the line of figure 6.1 again, then the total number of trips passing over every interval are given by the numbers below the line. These numbers assume that one trip is made from every point to every other. It is clear from this that the maximum volume of traffic passes the centre and that volume diminishes to a minimum at the periphery. Thus, the first piece of road should be built at the centre of the plain. As we have simplified things it could be built in any direction. Even if the authority did not reason in this fashion, they would undoubtedly have evidence of the volume of demand from the depth of ruts and the width of the muddied trace.

It seems intuitively proper that the next piece of road should go in at right angles to the first and that the network should be extended year by year from this cruciform central junction. This would extend the cost-reducing influence of the roadway most rapidly to the whole plain. The centrally located roads will further deepen the transport cost bowl and entrench grooves in it along the roads' alignments so that lines of equal travel cost will take on the shape in figure 6.2b.

Transport Networks and Economic Space

The geography of the transport network and its technical characteristics shape space differently from the Euclidean space of our uniform plain. Most theories of location depend on the geometry of homogeneous space. If we wish eventually to relate locational responses to transport investment we need to know the mapping between the even space of theory and the more complex space of transport networks. To clarify the matter, suppose that the tracks which farmers took on our plain were constrained and concentrated by the shape of fields and farms. The needs of the plough usually dictate a rectangular verge, thus, journeys would follow a recti-linear grid of paths. For convenience we can suppose them to be pointed east–west and north–south. In this case, the mapping from homogeneous to transport space is a well-known relationship. In figure 6.3, if a journey is made from i to j taking x miles from west to east and y miles from north to south, then the equivalent straight-line distance is given by $\sqrt{y^2+x^2}$. More generally this Pythagorean mapping may be written:

$$d_{ij}= s_{ij} (\sin \theta+\cos \theta)$$
where d_{ij} = network distance
s_{ij} = straight line distance
θ = the angular deviation of the straight line from the grid.

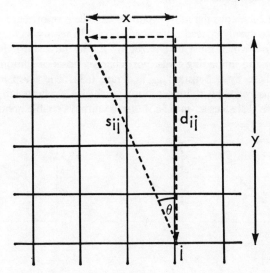

Figure 6.3

In much of our discussion of location, the argument was simplified by anchoring the economic space on one central focus and treating of transport costs and land price as they vary with distance from this focus. Travel costs will be expressed in terms of lines of equal travel cost or equal travel time, isotims or isochrones. In Euclidean space, if transport costs vary proportionally to distance, this map will consist of evenly spaced concentric circles, giving rise to an annular structure as in figure 6.4a. If the transport network is a rectangular grid with a uniform speed on all links with principal axes focused on the centre, then lines of equal travel cost will be square as shown in 6.4b. If speed on the principal axes of this network was twice that on local roads, then the isotims would be star-shaped as in 6.4c.

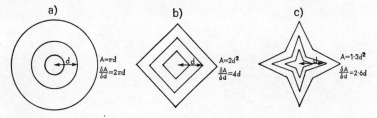

Figure 6.4

So far we have considered transport costs to be proportional to distance giving rise to evenly spaced isotims as in 6.5a. In reality there are usually terminal costs which must be covered no matter how short the journey, e.g. loading and unloading costs, port charges, costs of stations. We can represent these by a constant as in figure 6.5b. There are in addition economies associated with longer journeys which are reflected in a tapering of rates with distances as in 6.5c. Longer journeys enable greater vehicle

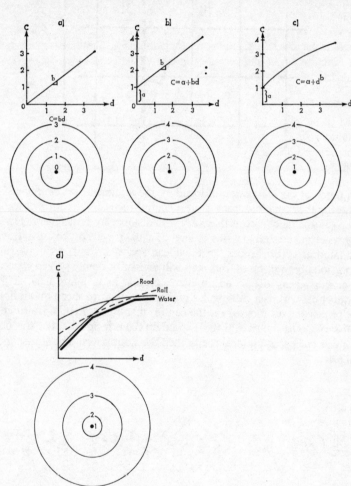

Figure 6.5

and labour productivity, spreading costs which vary with time, e.g. some element of wages, depreciation and insurance, over more miles. The shipper of goods is often faced with different means of transport to get to a given destination. Their varying technical characteristics give rise to different relationships of cost to distance, as suggested in figure 6.5d. Road carriage has small terminal costs and can offer the lowest charges per ton mile over short hauls. Truck mileage costs are high and after 200 miles or so the higher terminal charges of railways are offset by lower mileage costs and it becomes the lowest cost mode. If they are available, water carriers bear very high terminal costs but extremely low distance costs, so that they prevail as the lowest cost mode over long distances. The effective transport cost function for a shipper only interested in the per-ton-mile charge would be the lower envelope of all those as shown in 6.5d.

Transport Networks and the Supply of Land

If we wish to discuss the demand for land and its relation to transport costs we have to be able to determine the amount of land within a given transport cost limit and the rate at which this changes with distance from a fixed point. In the geometry of homogeneous space the area is given by πd^2 and the rate of change of area with distance from the focus is the circumference $2\pi d$. For the gridded space as in 6.4b, the area is $2d^2$ and the rate of change is the perimeter $4d$. For radials of twice the speed on the grid, as in 6.4c, the area is $1\cdot3d^2$ and the rate of change of area is $2\cdot6d$. Thus we can see that the transport network plays a critical role in defining the supply of space.

These constructions can be carried back to the relationship between price of land locations of activities and transport costs discussed in Chapter 2.

Lattice Networks

We have already dealt with a lattice network when we described a rect-angular grid of footpaths respecting the boundaries of square fields. We can, however, consider the nature of such a universal facility a matter of design. Suppose that the road authority of the plain were given a dual objective of achieving efficiency with geographical equity, i.e. bringing everywhere within some limited range of a road. Assume that there is no expectation of an increased concentration of activities, that demand is expected to remain fairly uniform for movement from any point to any other on the plain. The authority's task could be phrased in terms of providing a regular lattice network which minimizes the joint cost of construction and movement. Over the long run the network would be built up towards some regular network of roads covering the whole area. The design task then is to select which of the square, hexagonal and triangular networks is most efficient, these being composed of the only polygons which pack into a regular lattice. The first step is to standardize the access to roads in the plain. A reasonable design specification is that the average distance from the area contained in one element of the grid to the roadway is the same in each instance. It can be shown that in all three cases the average distance from the elementary area to a road is the same if the distance from the centre of the square, hexagon and triangle to the road (a in figure 6.6a, b and c) is the same. This is demonstrated in the Appendix.

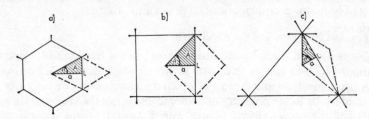

Figure 6.6

The next step is to calculate how these networks differ in the construction and maintenance costs they imply. If we can assume that there are no extra costs involved in building road crossings, which is perhaps not too unrealistic for the uncontrolled crossings of a rural network, then construction and maintenance costs will be proportional to the density of the network, i.e. the length of road per unit area of land. In all three networks the area served by one link is a rhombus as indicated by the dotted lines in figure 6.6 a, b and c. The angle 2θ will be 60°, 90°, and 30° for hexagon, square, and triangle respectively. Whatever this angle, the area associated with a length of road L will be La. Thus the density of network will be l/a miles per square mile and construction and maintenance the same for each. The choice between them consequently rests on the economy of movement costs they provide. Under the assumption of even demand for movement which we have made, this is a matter of calculating 'route factors', or the average divergence between any points, for the three networks. This has in effect been done already for the square lattice when we discussed how networks transform space. If we take the $d = s$ ($\sin \theta + \cos \theta$) relationship and average the values it gives over a 45° arc (since a square grid is symmetric in 8 such arcs) we obtain a route factor of $4/\pi$. This is the factor which straight-line distance must be multiplied by to give route distance. The calculations for hexagonal and triangular lattices are somewhat more complicated but similar in principle (see Appendix). The value for the hexagonal lattice is $4/\pi$ as well, whilst the triangular net has a much more favourable value of $2\sqrt{3}/\pi$. So there is nothing to choose between square and hexagonal grids and more to be said for the triangular grid. It is no wonder that we see diagonals cutting across square grids laid down for ease of surveying. The grid street pattern of Chicago could not submerge the rationale of old Indian trails that emerged radially from the portage between Lake Michigan and the Mississippi system and are to be seen in the likes of Ridge, Greenbay and Archer Avenues. The ring and radial structure we ascribe to the major routes of many cities, and indeed nations, could just as well be construed as a triangular lattice structure as in figure 6.7. For regular fine-grained use in congested urban networks the triangular grid does, however, present an engineer's nightmare of six-way junctions. Of all the square grid is probably the most natural and certainly the easiest to navigate about and survey. We do seem more at home with 90° than any other angle.

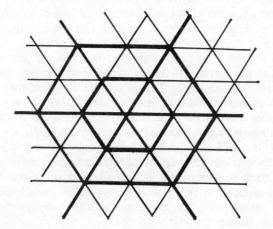

Figure 6.7

Route Location

In many instances towns emerged at some other fixed point than the centre of a plain, usually where commerce embarked and disembarked. From such coastal sites or riverine limits of navigation, routes were thrown inland to open access to agricultural or mineral resources. Such a scene

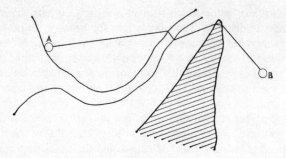

Figure 6.8

provides the occasion to discuss the choice of the best alignment for a
route between fixed points of travel demand. In figure 6.8 we have a port
located at A from whence a mining company desires to export copper ore
found in a rich lode at B. We assume that the size of the deposit and
expectations as to the gap between world copper prices and the cost of
extraction are sufficient to justify building a road to accommodate a given
number of truckloads a day. The company's engineer is given the task of
constructing a road so as to minimize the joint cost of construction and
trucking. On a homogeneous plain the solution is a straight line. But in the
figure we have placed a river and a range of hills in the way. The cost of
bridging a river is immensely higher per yard than that of laying road.
We would expect the route to refract so as to minimize the needed length
of bridge even though it added slightly to the length of the route from
A to B and increased transport costs. Since costs of earth-works, culverting
etc. are higher in hilly terrain than on the flat, one would expect a similar
tendency to avoid costlier upland construction to as great a degree as
possible. This must be balanced off against adding to the circuitry of the
route and the implied movement costs. It is not by chance that early trans-
American trails bent north through South Pass where the continental
divide is a gentle swell rather than drive straight through the Rockies'
saw-edged splendour as later rail routes and I70 have done since, with
construction costs comparatively reduced.

If we set aside the complications of the earth's physique we can introduce the added difficulty of joining three points such as A, B and C in
figure 6.9. Supposing the cost of movement vastly overwhelmed the cost
of construction then the best network would be a triangle joining A, B
and C directly. If the cost of construction is enormous and dominates the
decision then the minimum-length network in a 'Y' shape can be constructed as indicated in 6.9a. When allowance must be made, not only for some

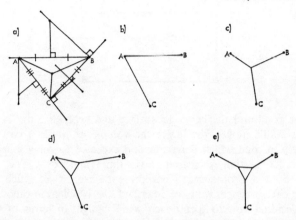

Figure 6.9

active trade-off between construction and movement costs, but also for different levels of demand to travel between the pairs of places, the problem gets very difficult to solve. If most of the movement is from *A* to *B* and from *A* to *C*, with little between *B* and *C*, and if construction costs are high relative to movement costs, a network like 6.9b might result. If there is a reasonable volume of movement between *B* and *C*, 6.9c is better. For a lower ratio of construction to movement costs, a network like 6.9d might meet the needs of this configuration of demand. If we now assume an even balance of demand, a shape like 6.9e would be the best. The difficulty with solving this problem mathematically is that you have to choose the right general shape or topology first before getting the details of length and location of junctions right. This is manageable for three points but becomes virtually impossible in joining four or more. The application of engineering and geographical intuition is called for.

Investment Appraisal

In some circumstances it is possible to specify a limited number of possible locations for links in a network. Then it becomes possible to set up the question of the best roads to build to meet some objective in a soluble fashion. In figure 6.10 there are five towns between which there is a given demand to travel. The road-building authority for the area has a fixed annual budget, determined politically. There are no physical barriers which could divert routes from the straight. The links drawn in the figure thus constitute all of the possible alignments. One question we have not addressed so far is that of route capacity. It must seem obvious that the

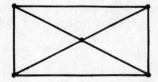

Figure 6.10

wider the road and the better its surface and geometry, the faster and smoother traffic moves, the larger the volume of traffic it can handle. Conversely, a road which is narrow and expected to carry much traffic will cause congestion, increased travel times and costs. The decision whether to build a route must incorporate the capacity at which to build it. In the circumstances we have described, the problem in time becomes one of deciding how to spend each year's budget in terms of building anew and expanding capacity of existing links so as to minimize the cost of travel. For small networks, measured by the number of links, this can be set up as a soluble mathematical problem. It can be formulated as a linear programming problem, i.e. finding the extreme value of a linear objective function determined by constraints limiting its extent in various directions.

So far we have assumed that demand for transport is either fixed or independent of route structure and capacity. Yet in Chapter 5 it was suggested that demand might well respond to increases in speed and reductions in distance. It is widely recognized that a new or improved route will not only serve those currently using it and divert some traffic from existing routes, but also generate new traffic. The problem actually faced by politicians and administrators is to take these effects into account when making additions or improvements to the existing capacity and structure. Even the Autobahnen, Interstates and Motorways were such, and not brand new independent networks laid down on a clean slate. The task becomes one of measuring the increment to national welfare resulting from a large number of possible projects, taking into account the interactions between the parts of the existing and proposed network and selecting those projects which maximize this increment. This can be formalized as a search for a building programme which maximizes welfare subject to a fixed budget or as a schema for calculating a rate of return on projects to compare with or meet the requirements of a central budgeting authority. In the U.K., for example, the Treasury requires that public works achieve a rate of return of over 10 per cent or produce a positive net benefit when streams of costs and benefits are discounted at 10 per cent per annum over their lifetime.

It is worthwhile clarifying a few points concerning investment at this juncture. By investing in roads or rolling stock, or any capital goods, we forgo present consumption in order to achieve increased consumption in the future. The net yield of this investment, the excess of future consumption over present consumption, does not attract funds without an additional inducement, because we have a preference for present over future consumption. The interest rate is the price which reconciles the productivity of capital with the preference for consuming now rather than later. We evaluate capital investments by transforming the stream of future benefits and costs that a piece of capital generates back to some present value. This involves discounting by the interest rate. A pound's worth of benefits to be enjoyed next year is not worth a pound now, even if we make an adjustment for inflation and are dealing in constant pounds. If the going rate of interest is 5 per cent and I put £0·95 aside now, it will grow to £1 in a year. Hence, the present value of £1 payable one year from now at a 5 per cent discount rate is £0·95. In general at interest rate i any principle grows at a rate of $(1+i)^t$, where t is the number of years. Inverting this gives us the expression for present discounted value of a pound's worth of cost or benefit arising t years from now:

$$\frac{1}{(1+i)^{t}}$$

In making investment decisions among a large number of different uses of limited funds, the golden rule is to act so as to achieve the largest present discounted value, selecting projects with the largest net present values. It is worth writing this out formally to be quite clear. We estimate the series of prospective costs k_t and benefits b_t of an investment over its lifetime of 1, 2, ... t, ... n years. Our general rule can be applied in three equivalent ways. We can select projects where:

$$\frac{b_1}{(1+i)^1} + \ldots + \frac{b_t}{(1+i)^t} + \ldots + \frac{b_n}{(1+i)^n} > \frac{k_1}{(1+i)^1} + \ldots + \frac{k_t}{(1+i)^t} + \ldots + \frac{k_n}{(1+i)^n}$$

or, alternatively, where:

$$\frac{\dfrac{b_1}{(1+i)^1} + \ldots + \dfrac{b_t}{(1+i)^t} + \ldots + \dfrac{b_n}{(1+i)^n}}{\dfrac{k_1}{(1+i)^1} + \ldots + \dfrac{k_t}{(1+i)^t} + \ldots + \dfrac{k_n}{(1+i)^n}} > 1$$

or, thirdly, if we define r to be the internal rate of return, given by the solution to:

$$\frac{b_1-k_1}{(1+r)^1}+ \cdots +\frac{b_t-k_t}{(1+r)^t}+ \cdots +\frac{b_n-k_n}{(1+r)^n}=0$$

then we should select projects where $r > i$.

The Components of Transport Benefits

We have already discussed the measurement of welfare associated with the use of transport facilities. Now we need to see how it is composed in the operation of a transport network, taking the effects on other parts of a network than the link proposed for building or improvement and effects on travel demand into account.

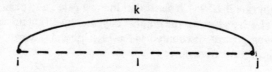

Figure 6.11

Let us start from the simplest configuration possible as shown in figure 6.11. This network consists of an origin i and a destination j linked by a somewhat circuitous existing road k on which the generalized cost of a trip is c_{ijk}. We consider investing in a new alignment between the two points labelled l. This will be more direct with better geometry and will thus have a lower cost of travel $c_{ijl} < c_{ijk}$. If the demand for travel is perfectly inelastic at T_{ij}^1 trips no matter the cost; if the volume travelling can never saturate the capacity of l and lead to congestion and if all travellers know and use the minimum cost route, then the change in consumer surplus brought about by building the new link would be: $T_{ij}^1 (c_{ijk}-c_{ijl})$, i.e. the saving in resource costs to existing users. If we allow for some responsiveness of demand to reduced travel costs, so that a greater demand $T_{ij}^2 > T_{ij}^1$, will result from the lower cost c_{ijl}, and if we can assume the demand curve for transport to be linear in the vicinity of the cost change, then the consumer surplus increase associated with this link will be:

$$\tfrac{1}{2} (T_{ij}^1+T_{ij}^2) (c_{ijk}-c_{ijl}).$$

Road system costs, and rail system costs, too, are governed by relationships between speed and flow, reflecting congestion effects. As flow increases beyond a certain point, so velocity falls. If we allow cost to increase with volume and assume that travellers are indifferent between routes of equal travel costs, then we can envisage an equilibrium where the costs on both routes will be equal and some travellers will be found on both links:

$$c_{ij} = c_{ijk} = c_{ijl} \text{ and } T_{ijk}{}^2 \text{ and } T_{ijl}{}^2$$

both occur. Under such circumstances the welfare change would have to be measured from both links:

$$\tfrac{1}{2} (T_{ij}{}^1 + (T_{ijk}{}^2 + T_{ijl}{}^2)) (c_{ijk} - \bar{c}_{ij}),$$

where $\bar{c}_{ij}$ is the equilibrium generalized cost after the adjustment in total volume and in choice between routes k and l has settled down.

It is evident that an evaluation of one project must consider the effects on competing routes and we can indicate this generally by writing the benefits expression as the sum over all route options between the origin and destination: $\tfrac{1}{2}\sum\limits_{k,l} (T_{ij}{}^1 + T_{ij}{}^2) (c_{ij}{}^1 - c_{ij}{}^2)$, where the superscripts refer to demands and costs with and without the project in question.

In reality we are usually faced with networks of many more than two nodes and we have to treat of complementarity as well as competition among routes. Roads l and k would usually be parts of paths connecting a great many other origins and destinations. Improvements between i and j will increase demand from further afield and thus affect costs on other links. For example, if the attractiveness of j as a centre for shopping is enhanced by building road l, then traffic may well be diverted from other stores, reducing demand and travel costs on routes serving them, and increasing volume and costs on links leading into j via i. Thus in order to capture the full effects of a network change, such as the building of l, changes in demand and generalized cost must be traced over all elements of the network affected. In dealing with urban roads especially, this has led some practitioners to do the calculations for all possible origins and destinations under the assumption that the intricacies of urban traffic and activities are so meshed that the whole system must respond and react to a change in any of its members. So the benefit of a scheme is estimated over all n zones in a town with:

$$\tfrac{1}{2} \sum_{i=1}^{n} \sum_{j=1}^{n} (T_{ij}{}^1 + T_{ij}{}^2) (c_{ij}{}^1 - c_{ij}{}^2).$$

The Geography of Transport Networks

To limit the extent of the estimation and calculation required by the above expression, we may search for geographical structure in terms of regions or fields of influence which contain the effects of any change. Since transport routes facilitate the motions of trade and travel which drive the economy, one would expect any geographical organization which the economy calls forth to be reflected in the arrangement of the transport system. The distinction between urban and rural is a fairly clear demarcation. We are quite happy to draw such a boundary around a town and, implicitly or explicitly, treat the rest of the road network as 'the rest of the world', pouring in a little traffic at a limited number of gateways. Everyday and political usage distinguishes 'regions' of a nation and in Chapter 9 we shall examine the functioning of regional economies. However, the definition of a 'regional' economy is not as obvious as the urban-rural limit. In practice arbitrary, administrative aggregations have been strung together to delimit a locality. Geographers have struggled long with defining and delimiting regions. At a broader scope the obvious escarpment of the urban-rural fringe is replaced by gentler economic gradients. Some sharp boundaries of soil and physique may be ameliorated by market circumstances and cultural homogeneity. The hinterlands of towns built to the specifications of rail and horse are blurred by the flexibility of the car and truck. However, the relationships between a major town and its hinterland, defined by trade and service connections, still offer a distinct possibility for the dismemberment of the national economy and its transport supports into partly autonomous entities which contain the benefits of any investment in facilities.

The most difficult task of partitioning is encountered in treating the intramural relationships of a town. Here, where the investment questions are most sensitive to the incidence of benefits and the repercussions of change most powerful politically and socially, the reality of independent regions and geographical limits is most questionable. Theorists have postulated annular, sectoral and multi-nuclear arrangements of activities within the city. The debate over which is correct continues unresolved. If particular cities were found to have sectoral structure this would imply a pattern of movement largely confined to wedges focused on the centre of town. Basically, it is difficult to divide up an urban road network because of the fineness of its mesh. It constitutes about 40 per cent of the urban area and could well be viewed as a continuous surface rather than a graph. Apart from barriers of rail and water which are sparsely penetrated by roads, lines of discontinuity in the town are bound to be impermanent and fuzzy. The interactions which transmit the effects of a transport improvement occur in competition for use of the road, not at places of origin and destination. The seemingly clear lines of land use and social demarcation become blurred when people seeking access to them compete for road space and routes. Because the cost the user bears is a function of the level of demand, the choice of activity locations as well as routes may be determined by the equilibrium which emerges from this competition for network capacity. The structure of a town is conditioned by the nature of its transport facilities. Locations for selling and producing different goods and for different types of dwelling are responses to the accessibility afforded by the means of transport and generate the surges of goods and people which employ their roads and tracks. It is, therefore, more valuable to examine the shape and use of the transport system directly than its shadow at one remove in the use of land.

Economic theorists have usually presumed an extremely simple network structure with a series of independent arteries radiating from one focus as in figure 6.2b. This collapses readily to two-dimensional diagrams and solutions. If we take this theoretical abstraction, allowing no connection between the radials, then there is no difficulty in breaking the net down into parts. Each sector associated with one radial operates independently of the other sectors. The only coordination is via the downtown focus. This transmits any result of changing one radius impartially to all others. Some actual networks, such as urban rail systems, do have a strong radial component with interstices between the branches broad enough to inhibit any interplay and, thus, may lend themselves to treatment as independent corridors.

At the other abstract extreme is the square grid of figure 6.3, serving a uniformly dense demand with trips being equally likely between all points. If this network is not subject to congestion, then the effect of increasing speed on any one link will be broadcast throughout the entire network. Before a change is made, all paths that get further from an origin and closer to a destination are of equal cost and thus would be used with equal likelihood. If the cost of traversing one link in such a set of paths is reduced, then all trips will divert to paths including the link and away from its competitors. Since we assume some travel from every part of the network to every other, then the diversionary effect will be felt everywhere. The reality lies somewhere between this extreme and that of independent radials. If congestion effects are operating in the square grid, so that speeds decline as volumes increase, then the perturbation caused by an improvement will dampen out with distance from the site of an improvement and eventually disappear. This waning has been observed in before and after studies of the emplacement of the Dan Ryan and Eisenhower Expressways in Chicago. The geographic peculiarities of the network in question obviously determine the precise form of attenuation of responses to road improvement.

There are two ways in which the question of satisfactory limits of geographical partiality for transport investment appraisal can be put. The first is whether a network can be divided into regions which encompass all the significant effects of any internal change. The second is where the limit of the sphere of influence of an individual link lies. If we have to evaluate a series of separate projects, then the sphere of influence formulation is more efficient, whereas if we were seeking the best programmes of additions to a national or town network from a large number of alternative combinations, the regionalization approach is the more appropriate. It may well be that the effects of any change on the rest of the system dampen out in a smooth fashion so that no discontinuities of the regional boundary type are discernible. In this case the limit of effects would be specified as a template centred on any particular project.

Congestion and Investment

We have alluded to congestion in road use. This presents a problem in investment appraisal because congestion represents a dead-weight loss of resources arising from a division between the result of private decisions and what is collectively best. Drivers in a congested system are not getting the right signals about the costs they are generating when they choose whether, where and when to travel. If we take a current excessive and inefficient level of demand as the basis for extrapolating the benefits of investment we are in danger of overestimating them.

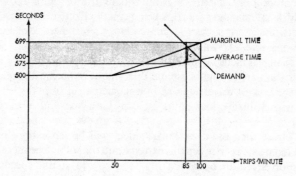

Figure 6.12

The loss due to congestion is most simply explored with a numerical example. Suppose there is a road between a housing estate and a football ground and that every Saturday before the start of the match drivers pour onto the road in a random fashion. The number who decide to enter the fray and make the trip is governed by a relationship with time taken, so that the shorter the expected time of travel the more will go. We will suppose that the time of travel can be judged by the speed of the traffic as it passes at the bottom of the street. If we plot the number of trips per minute against the travel time we get a downward-sloping curve of demand as in figure 6.12. The road is narrow and, after fifty cars per minute join the stream of traffic, the spacing between them reaches a critical point at which speed drops. This means that the average time taken for a trip increases, let us suppose by one second for each additional car. Drivers will continue to join the stream as long as the desire to go to the match for some people, expressed in the demand curve, exceeds the dissatisfaction of time forgone. When we get to the hundredth driver, his desire matches the time it will take him, the average travel time of 600 seconds. Now look at what his decision implies for everyone in the stream of traffic by finding the total travel time before and after he enters. For 99 cars the average time was 599 seconds giving a total of 59,301 seconds. For 100 cars the average time is 600 seconds and total time 60,000 seconds. The increment of time due to the marginal driver is thus 699 seconds. This is a familiar result of economics in a slightly different guise. Under increasing costs marginal cost exceeds average cost.

The relevant social cost is the marginal value which represents the change in the total consumption of time involved. Since drivers are only aware of average time, their private calculation of cost and benefit is generating a dead loss for society's budget of time equal to the shaded area in figure 6.12. What is needed to achieve the social optimum where demand and marginal time are equal, at 85 trips and an average of 575 seconds, is a signal to drivers to indicate the size of the imposition on others. A cash charge needs to be levied equal to the amount by which the marginal cost of travel exceeds the average cost (i.e. 75 seconds).

Reflection on the usual circumstances of congested travel, those of the daily journey to work, may cause hesitation over this prescription, however. Presuming that, over a week or so, the order in which travellers join the stream of traffic varies randomly, then it would be possible to argue that each traveller experiences the full range of travel times associated with the current volume on his route. Thus, the decision to travel is made in appreciation of the marginal cost of travel and the level of congestion on a route represents the socially optimal level of queueing.

A scheme of road pricing, charging motorists some approximation to marginal cost, taking into account levels of congestion by both time and place, has been proposed for U.K. cities. It is technically possible, if not feasible, to meter road use and record electronically charges which vary with the piece of road and velocity of traffic, as well as time of day. The cost of such a pricing mechanism might well exceed the loss of welfare it was instituted to remove, to say nothing of the political dissension it might rouse. Some cheaper proxies have been proposed and indeed applied. In 1974 Singapore instituted a system of daily licences for vehicles entering the central area of the city. Such an arrangement can hardly be fine-tuned enough and is bound to contain a large degree of arbitrariness. This could easily drive demand far below the socially acceptable level on many roads, thereby wasting socially useful capacity. One measure that seems appropriate in all circumstances is to shift any fixed element of motor taxes onto fuel, the consumption of which does increase with congestion. For most towns in the U.K. it does seem that if parking charges near the centre of town at least represented the opportunity cost of the land taken up and the cost of any structures involved, then traffic volumes could be held within socially acceptable limits. Parking is often directly or indirectly subsidized as local governments' attempts to maintain the drawing power of the capital sunk in their cores and clamour for more road capacity, or even rail capacity, to meet the inflated needs their policies encourage.

Road building in central urban areas of the U.K. and Europe does not appear capable of yielding an acceptable rate of return even if no adjustments are made to deflate for congestion. Given the density of occupation of these areas, other uses of land push the value of space beyond the reach of motorists. The Buchanan solution for growing traffic congestion in towns – a massive road-building programme to accommodate increasing demand for car travel to existing town structures – seems to have been a misplaced enthusiasm. The capacity of the existing system can be improved considerably by quite minor improvements in signalling and in the provision of queueing lanes at junctions, for it is at junctions that the capacity of a road is critically determined. Outside the dense city core there may be construction schemes worthy of attention. In suburbs of low density there is as yet no competition to road vehicles, car or bus, for meeting a rapidly diffusing pattern of travel needs. Plans to serve areas of low population density with a multiplicity of working, shopping, and playing focuses, with fixed rail transport, are to be counted in the realms of fantasy.

Throughout this chapter we have implicitly maintained the fiction that the demand for travel could be estimated as a function of land use and that this was given. A change in the volume of travel reflects a change in the intensity with which land is used. Our unfolding of the economy's geography brings us now to the point of predicting how people respond, in using land and locating activities, to changes in accessibility heralded by transport investments and innovations, relaxing an assumption of a known and immutable geography of production and consumption. This brings us full cycle in our partial analyses back to the theory of land use and value in Chapter 2.

Appendix

**Comparing Construction and Transport Costs
for Triangular, Square and Hexagonal Lattice Networks.**

(After the original by P. Melut and P. O'Sullivan, 'A comparison of simple
lattice transport networks for a uniform plain', *Geographical Analysis*, no. 6,
1974, pp. 163–73.)

Construction and movement costs in a regular network will depend on
the size of the elementary areas of the lattice. To compare networks which
are equally accessible to the population of a uniform plain, we can standardize them so that the expectation of the distance from a random point
on the plain to a link of the network is the same for each.

Taking the hexagonal network first, with a as the distance between the
centre of the elementary area and the network (figure 6.6a), for reasons of
symmetry the average distance to the network is the expectation of distance
to the edge of the polygon on the domain A (shaded). The area of A is
$a^2\sqrt{3}/6$. The average distance d_m to the network on A is the expectation of
$a-x$ for a uniform density. This is calculated by:

$$d_m = \frac{2\sqrt{3}}{a^2} \iint_A (a-x)\, dx\, dy$$

$$= \frac{2}{a^2} \int_0^a (a-x)\, x\, dx$$

$$d_m = a/3.$$

For the same reasons of symmetry we need only consider the average
distance on the domain A with summit angle $\pi/4$ for the square (figure 6.6b)
and $\pi/6$ for the triangle (figure 6.6c). The integration of the expectation of
distance on any domain A with summit angle θ gives the same result,

i.e. $\int_0^a (a-x) \left(\int_0^{\tan\theta x} dy \right) \frac{2dx}{a^2 \tan\theta} = \int_0^a \frac{2x\,(a-x)}{a^2}\, dx.$

Therefore, in all cases the average distance is $a/3$, and will be the same
when a is the same for each network.

We assume that construction and maintenance costs are proportional to the length of network per unit area. In all three networks in figure 6.7 the area served by one link is a rhombus with θ equal to $\pi/6$, $\pi/4$ and $\pi/3$ respectively. Whatever the value of θ, there will be a length of road L associated with an area La. Thus the density of network will be $1/a$ miles per square mile in all cases and construction and maintenance costs will be the same if a is the same for each network.

The only basis for discrimination among the networks then is movement costs which may be characterized by their route factors.

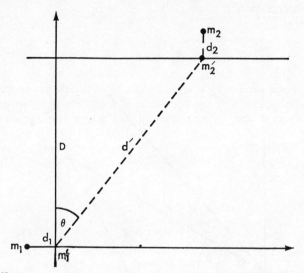

Figure 6.13

Consider two points m_1 and m_2 chosen at random on the plain, separated by a Euclidean distance d. With a square network as in figure 6.13, the shortest distance between them will consist of the overland distance d_1 from m_1 to m_1', the distance travelled along the network D and the overland distance from m_2' to m_2, d_2. In the square lattice the network distance is given by a simple transformation of the Euclidean distance d' from m_1' to m_2' along the azimuth θ: $d' \cos \theta + d' \sin \theta = D$.

Under the assumption that overland movement is infinitely more expensive than movement along the network, the expectation of $d_1 + d_2$ is $2 a/3$ in all three cases and we can ignore it and only consider D, reducing the problem to one of comparing route factors.

We write $D = d'r$ where d' is the Euclidean distance m_1' m_2' and r is called the route factor.

For reasons of symmetry it is only necessary to average the route factor between two main travel directions, i.e. for θ going from 0 to $\pi/2$ for the square and 0 to $\pi/3$ for the triangular and hexagonal networks.

For the square lattice:

$$r = |\cos\theta| + |\sin\theta|$$

therefore, the expectation of

$$r = R = (2/\pi) \int_0^{\pi/2} (\cos\theta + \sin\theta) \, d\theta$$

and R (square) $= 4/\pi$.

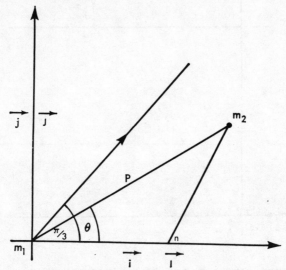

Figure 6.14

For the triangular network in figure 6.14

$$D = m_1 n + n m_2 \quad (\rho \text{ is constant})$$

$\overrightarrow{m_1 m_2}$ can be expressed as a linear combination of vectors $\overrightarrow{I}$ and $\overrightarrow{J}$ $((\overrightarrow{I}, \overrightarrow{J}) = \pi/3)$.

$$\left(\begin{array}{c} \overrightarrow{I} = \overrightarrow{i} \\ \overrightarrow{J} = \dfrac{\overrightarrow{i}}{2} + \dfrac{\sqrt{3}}{3}\overrightarrow{j} \end{array} \right) \Rightarrow \left(\begin{array}{c} \overrightarrow{i} = \overrightarrow{I} \\ \overrightarrow{j} = \dfrac{\sqrt{3}}{3}(2\overrightarrow{J} - \overrightarrow{I}) \end{array} \right).$$

Therefore,

$$\vec{m_1m_2} = \rho\cos\theta\,\vec{i}+\rho\sin\theta\,\vec{j} = \rho\left(\cos\theta-\frac{\sqrt{3}}{3}\sin\theta\right)\vec{i}+2\rho\frac{\sqrt{3}}{3}\sin\theta\,\vec{j}$$

and we have $D = \rho\left(\cos\theta+\frac{\sqrt{3}}{3}\sin\theta\right)$

or $r = \cos\theta+\frac{\sqrt{3}}{3}\sin\theta$.

Therefore, $R = \dfrac{3}{\pi}\displaystyle\int_0^{\pi/3}\left(\cos\theta + \frac{\sqrt{3}}{3}\sin\theta\right)d\theta$

$R\text{(triangle)} = \dfrac{2\sqrt{3}}{\pi}$.

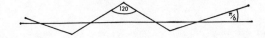

Figure 6.15

In the hexagonal case, only three directions of movement make $\pi/3$ angles with each other as in the triangular network, but travel in these directions along the network does not proceed along straight lines. As in figure 6.15, distance travelled is $1/\cos(\pi/6)$ times longer than the straight line and we have:

$$R\text{(hexagon)} = \frac{R\text{(triangle)}}{\cos\pi/6} = \frac{2\sqrt{3}}{\pi}\bigg/\frac{\sqrt{3}}{2}$$

$R\text{(hexagon)} = 4/\pi$.

Readings

The works by Meyer *et al.*, referred to at the end of the last chapter, spill over in scope to the subject of this chapter. The genesis of our present conception of transport supply and demand lies in: M. C. Beckmann, C. B. McGuire and C. B. Winsten, *Studies in the economics of transportation*, Yale University Press, New Haven, Connecticut, 1956.

Theory on planning of networks, however, goes back to at least A. M. Wellington, *The economic theory of the location of railways*, Wiley, New York, 1898.

The problem of network design is given an abstract geometrical treatment in M. C. Beckmann, 'Principles of optimum location for transport networks', in W. L. Garrison and D. F. Marble (eds), *Quantitative Geography*, vol. I, Northwestern University Studies in Geography, Evanston, Illinois, 1967, pp. 95–119.

Operational considerations are paramount in P. A. Steenbrink, *Optimization of transport networks*, Wiley, London, 1974. Congestion, and investment and pricing, is the subject of A. A. Walters, *The economics of road user charges*, The Johns Hopkins Press, Baltimore, 1968.

7. Realities of Doubt and Decision

Up to this point, the actors in our theories have for the most part been credited with omniscience. They have been imbued with perfect knowledge and perfect foresight. This assumption was relaxed when it came to understanding the competitive process among a few producers in a spatial market in Chapter 3. In that discussion, when making their moves, firms were conceived of as unsure of their competitors' likely responses and as sensitive to the certainty with which they could count on their share of the market. Such a characterization has a ring of reality about it which perfection lacks.

When we view the landscape we find it littered with a detritus of failures of foresight in locating productive capacity, transport facilities and social infrastructure. These artefacts of disequilibrium register the cost of ignoring or miscalculating the uncertainty which veils our knowledge of the world and its future. They are the wages of inflexibility. The imbalances of demand and supply visible in surplus and abandoned productive capacity and in congested facilities arise from unforeseen costs, climatic variations, and technical change, changes in the geography and magnitude of demand and changes in the tastes and preferences of consumers and the body politic. The realities of risk and uncertainty have shown themselves as quite sudden truncations of the continuity of expectations. Pools of jobless people around exhausted or superseded mines in Northumberland and Minnesota, outdated shipyards on the Clyde, and outdated coalfields and iron and steel works in Youngstown, Pennsylvania, bear witness to this, along with piles of wheat on the streets of Kansas towns. The history of transport is replete with radical switches between means of movement as technical advances provided new thresholds of advantage. Railways supplanted canals and in turn succumbed to the competition of trucks, cars and aircraft. Silted channels and overgrown tracks are the marks on the land of these discontinuities. The twice-daily metropolitan queues for road space and train seats evidence shortfalls of capacity.

One view of this question is a passive, descriptive one which attempts to explain the behaviour of people in the face of doubt and ignorance. Strategies in games of chance provide a close analogy for such circumstances. Responses and decisions can be appreciated as if they were moves in a game against a human opponent or against a fickle environment. The theory of games offers a rational explanation of many economic arrangements which appear less than the best when viewed in the naïve light of presumed perfect knowledge.

In the last chapter we made a switch from the description of economic behaviour to a more active, prescriptive attitude. Ways of making the best investment decision were sought. Continuing in that vein, we will here look at decision methods which reach for desired goals in such a fashion as to reduce the potential burden of uncertainty. In addition to dealing with fairly straightforward commercial desiderata, such as profit and market share, we must consider collectively-provided facilities where a broad definition of the public good must be employed and a correspondingly greater load of doubt must be borne.

The doubts which shadow a decision concern our understanding of the workings of the world and thus how it will change in the future. The second source of unease concerns the fixity of the preferences between various goods which the affected population do and will have. In practice these translate into uncertainties about cost, supply, demand and utility. Some examples will clarify the concern.

Environmental Changes

Apart from the uncertain certainty of death, man's most fundamental source of risk remains the weather. In either its slow change over a long haul, its annual perturbations or its sudden caprice, it can devastate man's hopes and calculations. Increasing aridity and the encroachment of desert desiccated the ancient economies of the Indus and the Tigris-Euphrates and the considerable society of the Pueblos of the Colorado Plateau prior to the thirteenth century. Prolonged drought and the work of man and his animals has recently spread the extent of unproductive land along the Sahel, the southern fringe of the Sahara, and through northern Ethiopia, bringing famine and pestilence. The periodic droughts which afflicted parts of the Great Plains in the late 1910s, the early 1930s, and early 1950s, and now in the late 1970s, reduced yields and incomes to nought in some places, causing considerable dislocation and hardship. Episodes of flood, fire, wind and snow have wreaked widespread or localized havoc with the expected product of work and the cost of living.

Cost Instability

It was remarked in Chapter 2 how technical change in steel-making has reduced the cost of the coal used. With depleting reserved, the price of oil-derivative fuels may well mount relative to other goods used for either production or consumption activities. A drop in the cost of transfer from sea transport to land carriage, with container, roll-on roll-off and barge-shedding ships, has made much of the world's port capacity redundant, decentralized the points of land–sea egress or break of bulk and diffused overland flows of traffic.

Misapprehensions of Demand

There have been big and sudden switches in the order of preference among goods which a national market displays. In the U.S.A. after the First World War the demand for salad vegetables suddenly appeared and soared, replacing potatoes, greens and roots in the national diet to a considerable degree. The geography of demand reflects that of jobs, which may change with the relative advantage of locations for production. As the location and type of consumption and production change, so the demand for transport by a particular means or between particular places may surge or plummet quite at odds with naïve extrapolations of current trends. The build-up of demand for coal movement in Britain's Industrial Revolution swamped the capacity of the natural waterways that served as her veins up to the early eighteenth century. In the early 1970s predictions of exponential growth in air travel were shown to be mistaken when passenger numbers proved to increase along a logistic path, leaving many airlines with an excess of capacity. The secularity of this trend was disproved in 1978 when traffic surged in response to lowered prices. A blatant example of patently false hopes is visible in the plans for development of local governments. In the U.K. the sum of local authorities' expectations as to central area office employment, and thus commuter volumes, far exceeds any reasonable estimate of total national employment in this category. These excessive prospects then fuel local bids for central government funds to subsidize rail services or build up road capacity.

Evolving Tastes, Fashion and Notions of Well-being

Perhaps the most perplexing component of insecurity in making choices now for future satisfaction lies in the worth we attach to various goods and bads. The calculation eventually comes down to specifying the elements and their relative importance which combine to form the objective criterion with which we judge the balance of costs and needs implied by various courses of action. What is involved is the constitution of the social welfare function and the preference accorded to different things now and in the future.

The working out of changes in values can be seen in the politics of energy policies. The direction of such a policy must be governed by the compromise which is reached between the needs for cheap heat and power, security of supplies of energy, acceptable pollution levels, willingness to savage the landscape or undertake the risks involved in the production of nuclear energy and so on.

In urban transport planning, a switch in the 1960s from engineering concepts of efficiency to the economists' maximization of consumer surplus did much to change the accent of solutions. The achievement of some performance standards was replaced by the balance of a discounted stream of generalized cost of travel savings against the present value of construction and maintenance costs. As the economizing of cash and time gives way in weight to collective, environmental requirements, so the objective of the planning exercise and thus a good design changes. With a deeper appreciation of the interwoven relations between land use and transport, there is acceptance of a more all-embracing appraisal of potential lost opportunities. The soundness of more simply-motivated choices becomes questionable. These matters are subject to the quirks of fashion, especially as people respond to political dramatizing. Thus, the 'environmental' goods whose value rose through the 1960s in comparison with that of the ease of travel suffered, after 1973, an erosion of worth in favour of energy efficiency. These historical instances of evolving consciousness and changing sensibilities indicate the uncertainty which exists over the goals of investment.

Investment Practice

In practice, ignorance of the future has been dealt with according to the mood of the time. Expansionist optimism took leaps in the dark, catering for unknown potential by lavish over-provision. In more austere circumstances, dour frugality suffers the unexpected as the cost of bottle-necks and shortages.

When degrees of uncertainty can be distinguished, degrees of arbitrary conservatism have been employed. Pessimistic benefit forecasts have been taken if the danger was seen to lie in the erosion of demand over time. Premiums were placed on discount rates according to riskiness which was perceived to compound with time. The life-span over which benefits and costs are discounted was curtailed from an engineering estimate if it was felt that the danger was of a sudden truncation of benefits, due to obsolescence, say.

In addition to these ad hoc, judgemental allowances for risk, sensitivity analysis is a practical tool often employed. The method involves varying the assumptions made about future streams of benefits and costs between pessimistic and optimistic extremes and investigating how responsive the return on the investment is to such variations.

Discount rate, 'writing down' and life-span adjustments all involve the arbitrary selection of some value. Sensitivity analysis treats the effect of departures from some most likely state of affairs one at a time. This may mislead judgement, for the reality may involve a compound of departures in both directions, among many variables.

Characteristic Decision Circumstances

We have ascribed the doubts which haunt decision to two general sources. There is the doubt which stems from lack of knowledge about the causes of things and consequent lack of ability to predict the outcome of possible actions. The other source concerns the apprehension of present and future preference ordering among potential outcomes.

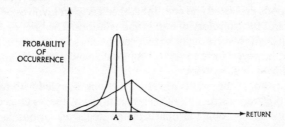

Figure 7.1

The doubt we have about our knowledge of these two questions is a matter of degree. For convenience of expression we can distinguish three points from this continuum of dubiousness. At one end of the spectrum 'certainty' implies the ability to determine an outcome precisely. In figure 7.1, if this were the case, we could use the point estimates of the returns to two projects at A and B, in which case B is unambiguously better than A. 'Uncertainty' can be taken to mean that we can put odds of varying degrees of precision on the likelihood of a particular outcome. In the figure we show probability distributions of outcomes distributed about the central estimates of A and B. As drawn, B is a riskier proposition and there is some likelihood that it will fare far worse than A or vastly better. A, with a tight distribution of possible values, is a much surer thing. The condition where any such numerical grading of possible states of the world would be spuriously exact we designate 'ignorance'. We may be able to identify the possible values which the returns to A and B might take and specify their range, but we cannot put a likelihood on them.

Falling out of these categories of sources and types of uncertainty there are combinations of circumstances under which different approaches to the decision-making problem will be appropriate.

If there is certainty about the outcomes of courses of action open and certainty about the value of the outcomes and costs involved, then the decision problem becomes a purely computational one. Suppose the circumstances were as described in the blast-furnace example in Chapter 2, so that the extent of the market, price and cost of all locations were known, then finding the best site is a matter of calculation. As we saw, for all that we know of the existence of a unique best solution to such a problem, it may still be a cumbersome matter to figure which it is from a vast array of possibilities. In effect some range of the axis of returns in figure 7.1 is continuously occupied by possible locations.

If our knowledge of causal structure and outcomes is limited but we are certain of the preferences of the clientele of the action between the various goods produced and employed, then decision involves professional judgement of the trajectory of events and relations. The brief of a manager of a firm from its owners might be to locate plants so as to maximize profits. He might, however, have to predict future demand and costs and exercise his expertise in these matters.

Certainty about the results of various actions, coupled with uncertainty as to the preference structure of their constituency, makes choice a search for compromise among the unarticulated goals of various factions. In the discussion of congestion in Chapter 6, it might be that the workings of the system are quite well understood but that wide disparities existed over the value of time to adopt in marginally costing use of a congested facility. The rich might prefer to pay and the poor to wait in line.

When both causality and the ranking of preferences are matters of ignorance, then what is called for is inspirational leadership or random improvisation. Although for simplicity we may talk in certainties and probabilities, if we are honest this characterizes reality more often than we admit.

Planning under Uncertainty

As a first step in varying the degrees of conviction about values and processes involved in investment planning we may assume that it is legitimate to construct subjective probability distributions over outcomes of options open to the planner, such as those about A and B in figure 7.1.

If the decision-maker is not averse to risk then he can work simply with the mean values of the distributions as expected values of outcomes and ignore the variance of results. In many circumstances, however, there is some aversion to taking risk, so that some trade-off must be established between the mean and variance of outcomes. If the decision-maker can specify this trade-off, then it can be incorporated in a decision calculus which selects the outcomes maximizing expected utility.

Decisions with Limited Foresight

We assumed above that we had sufficient knowledge to compute the probability of various configurations of demand and performance associated with particular courses of action. This would often be a ludicrous requirement and it would be better honestly to plead ignorance. There is a step between having precise knowledge of probability density functions of outcomes and the admission of complete ignorance. Sufficient information may exist to rank the likelihood of future states of the world. If the pay-offs, or net present values, associated with certain actions are known, then it is possible to calculate the minimum and maximum expected pay-offs for any single investment strategy to use in making a choice.

Decision-making under Ignorance

There are several general ploys available when we cannot judge the likelihood of future states of the world on any cardinal or ordinal scale, but know the pay-off associated with each possible combination of action and state of the world.

The Bayes or Laplace criterion assigns equal probabilities to each of the possible outcomes and uses these to compute the expected value of each action, so as to select the maximum. However, the results obtained do depend on the number of equally likely outcomes identified.

The Minimax approach goes to the conservative extreme of determining the worst possible outcome for each option available. The action with the highest minimum value is then selected, thus maximizing the worst possible gains. This is the strategy of purest cowardice, which in some circumstances may be the most rational. The Maximax strategy goes for the long shot, appealing to more heroic, and potentially dangerous, instincts by selecting the project with the largest maximum pay-off.

To balance out these two tendencies a weighted average of maximum and minimum values, called the Hurwicz criterion after its progenitor, may be used. This implies an arbitrary judgement of weights.

The Minimax criterion can be applied to a measure of the regret or opportunity cost associated with a decision turning out wrong. Regret is measured as the difference in pay-offs between pairs of action-state combinations. Thus, it registers what is forgone for any action-state realization by the action chosen.

These ignorance criteria can yield completely different best choices. This is made clear by the pay-off matrix in figure 7.2. The first action is best according to the Bayes strategy, the second according to Minimax, the third if Hurwicz's criterion is used with a weighting for extreme values

OUTCOMES

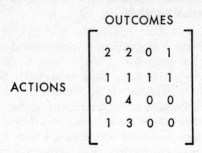

ACTIONS

Figure 7.2

of over a quarter or if Maximax is applied, and the fourth if the minimum value of the maximum regret is used.

Flexibility as an Objective

The illustration of divergence of choice in figure 7.2 points up the power of subjective differences in determining what is best. Forcing the circumstance of decision into a simple extremum-seeking mould, employing deterministic optimizing methods, conceals but cannot satisfy the real requirement for expression of attitudes and allowance for their play in the selection of appropriate actions. The over-rigid specification of a long-term goal makes things tidy, but possibly silly.

Decisions are most frequently made in a continuing sequence. A structure evolves from the sequential addition of pieces. The location of plants of a many-plant firm usually represents an historical series of decisions. A road network is built up a link at a time. It is possible to modify the geographical configuration which is emerging as new information is unearthed and better understanding of the processes and needs involved flourishes. It is not necessary to commit the system inevitably to a particular future shape. Distinguishing between a plan and a decision, it is only a decision and action which represent an irreversible commitment of resources. A plan is a set of prospective dated decisions which may be reversed or revised prior to their due date, in the light of new knowledge or changed circumstances.

In recognition of these realities, 'robustness' has been put forward as a decision criterion for sequential decision-making under conditions of ignorance. This quality is defined as 'useful flexibility'. In statistics 'robustness' implies insensitivity to assumptions. From this usage the meaning of the term when applied to decisions is clear. A collection of decisions whose rude health will enable them to perform well, no matter what befalls, makes a flexible plan.

The criterion is intended for use in planning facilities where probabilities cannot be assigned to the future behaviour of customers, competitors, input providers and government and their attitudes and priorities. It is to be expected that the train of unpredictable and ungovernable events surrounding the activity in question will be accompanied by an increasing awareness of what the desired future might consist of. This may occasion adaptation of any plan, which can be done by changing the uncommitted stages of the plan. If the possibility of such modification is not built into the planning framework and did not influence the early decisions taken, then there may be insufficient play in the structure to respond to the improved perception of needs and goals. Any choice limits the future by committing the present. A plan whose first steps limit the future as little as possible has an evolutionary advantage in a life beset with uncertainty.

The quality of robustness has to be quantified for operational use. For a firm which produces in several geographically dispersed plants, there are a finite number of sites at which production could be expanded, considering both *in situ* expansion and green-field locations. At any time a decision in favour of building or expanding plant i can only be made for a limited number of the potential sites. The future may be conceived of as a set of maps S of actions and states of the world, of which one will be realized in the long run. Any present decision in favour of site i will restrict the attainable futures to a sub-set S_i of S. For some sub-set $\bar{S}$ of the maps S, which are judged 'good' final outcomes on the variety of criteria involved, a sub-set $\bar{S}_i$ will still be available after the present decision in favour of i. Then the useful flexibility of the expansion of productive capacity at i is given by:

$$f_i = \frac{(\bar{S}_i)}{(\bar{S})}.$$

Present steps in a sequence of decisions should be chosen so as to maximize this quantity, switching the emphasis from a final plan to continuous planning.

Successful design has always implicitly incorporated robustness in long-lived things. Structures were erected to meet dimly foreseeable contingencies at a minimum cost and yet to serve immediate needs quite well. The evolutionary process favours adaptable things of high tensile strength. Platonic specialization and related notions of optimality are doomed for violating the enjoinder 'Nothing too much.' Political traditions and social *mores* have succeeded best where they fostered generality and avoided over-specialization to ensure long-term stability, as prescribed by Aristotle. Flexibility and resilience of structure are attained by having rugged components which can easily adapt to new circumstances. Robustness as a criterion formalizes a sound conservative tendency to discount the arrogance of over-simplification, displaying a more truthful humility in respect of what is known and what is knowable.

Readings

The classic on uncertainty is F. H. Knight, *Risk, uncertainty and profit*, Houghton Mifflin, Boston, 1921.

M. J. Webber discusses the geographical implications in *Impact of uncertainty on location*, Harvard University Press, Cambridge, Massachusetts, 1972.

The robustness criterion is propounded, using a plant-location problem by way of example, by J. Rosenhead, M. Elton and S. K. Gupta in 'Robustness and optimality as criteria for strategic decisions', *Operational Research Quarterly*, no. 23, 1972, pp. 413–31.

8. General Economic Equilibrium and Geography

Up to now, the solutions to theoretical problems have been based on assumptions about the constancy of a number of the phenomena involved. Production was located given its proximity to a market and the supply of transport. Residences were located with respect to a given work-place and transport system. The best transport network was determined for a given disposition of activities and demand for transport. The question naturally arises whether we can dispense with this partial approach and make some statements about the operation of the economy's geography when everything is allowed to vary simultaneously. It is an item of the economist's creed that everything is related to everything else. The economy is seen as a fully connected whole in which a multiplicity of individual decisions to consume and produce goods are coordinated by an in-built mechanism of social control. An external impulse perturbing the quiet of the arrangement in one place will be spread throughout via the interlocking relations of buyers and sellers. The final configuration of prices and quantities, after all the needs and resources of society have been balanced, will be a new, general equilibrium. Over the last century Adam Smith's figurative 'invisible hand' has been transformed into mathematical statements of the balance arising between the material desires of men and the limited means at their disposal. The solution of a set of simultaneous equations can be interpreted as the conditions under which an economy achieves a steady state. The equations specify the structure of markets, technology and the motives of people's behaviour. If the connections between buyers and sellers can be expressed in as many equations as unknown variables, then the values of the variables which satisfy all the equations simultaneously represent their equilibrium levels. To be geographical, the specification of the balance must have the dimensions of distance and direction. The places of production and consumption should be determined and a transport industry carrying trade between locations should be included.

A Simple Exchange General Equilibrium

A simple, non-geographical case will make the nature of general equilibrium formulations clear. Suppose the economy in question is a small town where transport costs are negligible. The town is merely a market where n commodities are bought and sold. The quantity of each good demanded d_i is a function of a constant representing the effect of consumer tastes a_i plus a linear combination of its own price p_i plus the prices of all other goods p_j, as substitutes or complements:

$$d_i = a_i + b_{i1}p_1 + \ldots + b_{ii}p_i + b_{ij}p_j + \ldots + b_{in}p_n$$

where the b_{ij}'s are coefficients indicating the influence of the price of good j on the demand for good i. The supply of each commodity s_i is governed by a constant representing production technology e_i plus a linear combination of the influence of its own price and all other prices:

$$s_i = e_i + f_{i1}p_1 + \ldots + f_{ii}p_i + f_{ij}p_j + \ldots + f_{in}p_n$$

where the f_{ij} represent the effect on the supply of i of the price of good j. Writing these equations out for the demand and supply for each commodity we characterize the workings of the economy in $2n$ equations:

$$d_1 = a_1 + b_{11}p_1 + \ldots + b_{1n}p_n$$

$$\cdot \quad \cdot \quad \cdot \quad \quad \cdot$$
$$\cdot \quad \cdot \quad \cdot \quad \quad \cdot$$
$$\cdot \quad \cdot \quad \cdot \quad \quad \cdot$$

$$d_n = a_n + b_{n1}p_1 + \ldots + b_{nn}p_n$$

$$s_1 = e_1 + f_{11}p_1 + \ldots + f_{1n}p_n$$

$$\cdot \quad \cdot \quad \cdot \quad \quad \cdot$$
$$\cdot \quad \cdot \quad \cdot \quad \quad \cdot$$
$$\cdot \quad \cdot \quad \cdot \quad \quad \cdot$$

$$s_n = e_n + f_{n1}p_1 + \ldots + f_{nn}p_n.$$

For ease of manipulation this may be rewritten in the form of matrices of coefficients and vectors of variables and constants. Defining:

$$d = \begin{bmatrix} d_1 \\ \cdot \\ \cdot \\ \cdot \\ d_n \end{bmatrix} \quad s = \begin{bmatrix} s_1 \\ \cdot \\ \cdot \\ \cdot \\ s_n \end{bmatrix} \quad p = \begin{bmatrix} p_1 \\ \cdot \\ \cdot \\ \cdot \\ p_n \end{bmatrix} \quad a = \begin{bmatrix} a_1 \\ \cdot \\ \cdot \\ \cdot \\ a_n \end{bmatrix} \quad e = \begin{bmatrix} e_1 \\ \cdot \\ \cdot \\ \cdot \\ e_n \end{bmatrix}$$

$$B = \begin{bmatrix} b_{11} & \ldots & b_{1n} \\ \cdot & & \cdot \\ \cdot & & \cdot \\ \cdot & & \cdot \\ b_{n1} & \ldots & b_{nn} \end{bmatrix} \quad F = \begin{bmatrix} f_{11} & \ldots & f_{1n} \\ \cdot & & \\ \cdot & & \\ \cdot & & \\ f_{n1} & \ldots & f_{nn} \end{bmatrix}.$$

We can write:

$$d = a + Bp$$

and $s = e + Fp$.

This system is equilibriated by a set of prices which equate the demand and supply for each commodity. The solution vector of prices can be obtained by setting supply equal to demand:

$$s = d.$$

This implies:

$$a + Bp = e + Fp$$

which rearranges to:

$$(B - F)p = e - a.$$

To get the relevant quantities this is substituted into the original demand equation to give:

$$d = B(B - F)^{-1} (e - a) + a$$

and, since at equilibrium demand equals supply, the same quantities hold for supplies. Given the coefficients and constants, by finding the inverse $(B - F)^{-1}$ we can obtain prices which balance all supplies and demands, taking all own-price and cross-elasticities of demand and supply into account.

Utility-maximizing Equilibrium

This construction is not very rich in motive and behaviour, assuming them as given constants and coefficients. It merely balances quantities. We usually think of people in the role of economic actors as seeking a set of purchases and sales which is best in terms of a measure of worth. The producer is seen as motivated by profit maximization. This can, however, be dispensed with as a complicating factor by assuming that markets are perfect, consisting of large numbers of buyers and sellers with perfect knowledge and foresight, so that profits will be driven to zero, prices will equal marginal costs and entrepreneurial decisions will be redundant. This leaves the consumers' motive as a maximand for the economy. Consider a society of m individuals j ($j = 1 \ldots m$) whose behaviour is governed by utility functions expressing the worth they obtain from holding combinations of the n commodities i ($i = 1 \ldots n$) available. They seek to maximize this utility by their purchases and sales. The commodities consist of two groups. Firstly, there are factors of production labelled $s = 1 \ldots k$. Then there are consumer goods labelled $t = k+1 \ldots n$. The state of rest of the economy will be described by nm values for the quantity of good i held by individual j, Q_{ij}; by k quantities of factors of production used Y_s; by $n-k$ final good outputs Y_t and $n-1$ prices. The price of one good will be taken as unity ($p_n = 1$) and all prices will be expressed in proportion to this. Thus we have a total of $nm+2n-1$ unknown values for which we wish to solve.

We may write individual j's utility function as follows:

$$U_j = f_j (Q_{1j}, Q_{2j}, \ldots, Q_{nj}).$$

This can be thought of as a hill in n dimensional commodity space. The individual seeks to maximize his utility by climbing up the gradient towards the crest of the hill where gradients become zero. The gradient, or the rate at which utility changes as the quantity of any good held increases, is given by the partial derivative of this function with respect to the good in question:

$$u_{ij} = \frac{dU_j \ (i = 1 \ldots n)}{dQ_{ij} \ (j = 1 \ldots m)}.$$

The individual is inhibited from reaching the top of the hill, and from driving these derivatives to zero, by the limit of his income. He can only buy goods with income he earns from sales of his holdings, $\bar{Q}_{ij}$, one of which is labour or leisure. The budget constraint on the individual is that expenditures equal income which may be put as:

$$\sum_i p_i (Q_{ij} - \bar{Q}_{ij}) = 0 \quad \text{for } j = 1 \ldots m. \qquad \ldots 1$$

In seeking to maximize their utility subject to these constraints, people will equate prices to marginal utilities. At equilibrium for any two goods the ratio of their marginal utilities should equal the ratio of their prices:

$$\frac{u_{ij}}{u_{nj}} = \frac{p_i}{p_n}$$

but since $p_n = 1$ then:

$$u_{nj} = \frac{u_{ij} \ (i = 1 \ldots n-1)}{p_i \ (j = 1 \ldots m)}. \qquad \ldots 2$$

The production side of the economy is assumed to be innocent of increasing or decreasing returns to scale, so that the relationship between the output of industry t and the input of factor s is given by a fixed co-efficient g_{st}, the amount of factor needed per unit output. The amounts of factors of production sold by individuals at equilibrium will be given by the sum of consumer goods outputs times these coefficients for all inputs:

$$\sum_t g_{st}\, Y_t = -Y_s\ (s = 1 \ldots k).\qquad\qquad \ldots 3$$

Obviously, in the final balance, supplies and demands summed over all individuals must be equal. The total purchase of a commodity is:

$$Q_i = \sum_j Q_{ij}.$$

The initial holding over all individuals is:

$$\bar{Q}_i = \sum_j \bar{Q}_{ij}.$$

For factors of production the difference $\bar{Q}_s - Q_s$ is the amount used in production. For consumer goods the excess of purchases over initial holdings $Q_t - \bar{Q}_t$ is the necessary level of new production. The market balance then is met by:

$$Y_i = Q_i - \bar{Q}_i\ (i = 1 \ldots n-1).\qquad\qquad \ldots 4$$

The values in one of the n equations of this kind are determined by the sum of the others; thus only $n-1$ equations need solutions. Since we have assumed perfect competition and constant production costs, then prices of consumer goods in this formulation will equal costs thus:

$$\sum p_s g_{st} = p_t\ (t = k+1 \ldots n).\qquad\qquad \ldots 5$$

With m equations of type 1, $m(n-1)$ of 2, k of 3 ,$n-1$ of 4, and $n-k$ of 5, we have as many equations, $nm+2n-1$, as unknowns. If we knew the nature of the utility functions f_j, production coefficient values and initial holdings of goods, it is possible that unique solutions could be simultaneously found for prices, outputs, purchases and usage of factors of production.

Inter-regional General Equilibrium

Our next step is to inquire if geography can be incorporated in such a structure. The most complete manner of doing this would be to give the eastings and northings of each producer and consumer, tagging each variable with a cartesian index, xy, which becomes a variable itself. This is obviously impractical. In addition, in mathematical terms it introduces the basic intractability we discussed in connection with industrial location. What can be done is to categorize geographical space by designating a set of regions. These are taken to be punctiform, like the nodes of a network.

Relations between regions can be viewed as taking place along the limbs of a network. Transport costs are incurred in connecting buyers and sellers at two nodes but not if they are at the same node. Continuous geographical space is transformed to the discrete space of a graph which can be addressed with finite mathematics. The quantities of the economy now take on a regional designation. If we have r regions ($a = 1, 2, \ldots a, b, \ldots r$), then the quantities of goods can be labelled:

$$Q_{ij}{}^a \text{ or } Y_t^b.$$

The fact that regions may differ in their resource bases can be represented by differences in production coefficients so that

$$g_{st}{}^a \rightleftharpoons g_{st}{}^b.$$

This gives rise to regional differences in consumer good prices and thus the potential for inter-regional trade. In determining the equilibrium level of trade between two places T_t^{ab}, then the conditions we described in Chapter 5 must obviously prevail. The price difference between any two trading regions must just equal the unit cost of transport between them c_t^{ab}:

$$p_t^a + c_t^{ab} = p_t^b.$$

In addition, the quantity imported must equal the quantity exported:

$$T_t^{ab} = -T_t^{ba}.$$

These conditions ensure that there is no cross-hauling of identical goods so that there will be a maximum of $\frac{r(r-1)}{2}$ shipments among r regions. If we assume that, for the period of analysis, factors of production are geographically immobile, then each region's factor requirements will be governed internally by:

$$Y_s^a = Q_s^a - \bar{Q}_s^a.$$

Consumer goods may, however, be traded; thus in any region differences between holdings and purchases may be made up by a trade balance:

$$Y_t^a = Q_t^a - \bar{Q}_t^a + \sum_{\substack{b=1 \\ b \neq a}}^{r} T_t^{ab}.$$

Introducing these relations in a manner which leaves a soluble set of as many equations as unknowns might make it possible to solve for regional production, consumption, and prices, and the flows of goods between regions. These flows would translate into demands placed on the transport industry.

General and Partial Models

The graph of regional nodes and linear links with which we must portray the economy to achieve mathematical manageability is a far call from the economic landscape in which we experience its fortunes. A great deal more detail has to be surrendered in such a general model than can be represented in a partial model. The best understanding is to be had by changing resolution between a microscopic examination of local intricacies and then a blurring of the finework to gain an impression of the whole ensemble within which the issue of interest is embedded. It is desirable when analysing some part of the economy to remind yourself of the 'other things' which will be considered 'equal' and their potential volatility. Whether to apply a general or partial approach to solving a problem depends on whether the changes involved are localized or whether they are likely to reshape the network of prices and quantities in the economy. For the evaluation of limited public-work projects a partial appraisal is usually sufficient. A change in the tax structure will need a more general appraisal.

Operational Forms of General Equilibrium

In order to apply the notion to problems in the real world it is necessary to deal in observable relations, calculable proportions and instrumental variables susceptible to political control. One means to bring complexity within manageable bounds is aggregation. This is how Keynes's General Theory was phrased, collapsing the mass of individual purchases of goods and factors into the aggregate variables, consumption and investment. The utility-maximizing drive of the system outlined above is replaced in Keynes's theory by the observed regularity of the propensity to spend or save increased income. In Chapter 9 this macro-economic structure is applied to a regional economy and its relations with other regions.

A large number of commodities can be specified in a general model if the connections between parts of the economy are reduced to extreme simplicity. Leontief's input–output analysis, which will also be treated in Chapter 9, rules out utility functions in favour of exogenously given final demands. The same constant production coefficients assumed above then yield a readily soluble system of linear equations.

If we can express the driving force of the economy in more specific and measurable terms than utility maximization, then mathematical programming methods can be used to compute equilibria. Given a concern with the geographical disposition of activities it might be that we can express an efficiency objective in terms of the minimization of transport costs over the entire economy. If these could be construed as a linear combination of per-ton-mile charges and ton-miles moved, the whole could be set up as a variant of the Transportation Problem in linear programming, which is readily soluble.

A final operational mode of general modelling involves casting aside the notion of equilibrium in order to explore complex interactions. Instead of solving a system for its state of rest, the complicated relations are simulated in a probabilistic manner. A trajectory of change is predicted by drawing events at random from probability functions describing the relevant processes. This trajectory can be examined for its stability or volatility and the expected outcomes of any disturbances forced on it. Such simulation exercises are, however, prone to appear as numerical manifestations of their author's prejudices.

The Geographical Limits of Partiality

The selection of a fine or coarse resolution for the examination of an economic problem can be a question of geography. In fact we may consider the classical statements of general equilibrium in economics to be partial insofar as they ignore location and transport costs, balancing the economy on a pinhead. The eighteenth-century British economy moulded the classical works of economics. This was limited in its geographical sweep and laced with estuaries and waterways, so that a single market unhindered by distance friction was a reasonable abstraction. The shares of land, labour and capital, wheresoever they accrued, were the outstanding social issues. Increasing political sensitivity to territorial rather than class constituencies in the U.K. has led to efforts to remedy the 'Anglo-Saxon space-less bias' and appreciate the geographical workings of the economy. In the U.S.A., which is larger and has a greater disparity of climate and physique and with a stronger constitutional embodiment of territorial representation the populations of the different sections have long done battle for their several economic interests, with guns, laws and finance. It is not surprising that a keener interest in urban and regional issues developed among American economists, looking to the plains of Mecklenburg and the downlands of South Germany as well as the City of London for theoretical inspiration. This was the genesis of Regional Science with a mission to insert space into economics and general equilibrium theory in particular.

Such considerations aside, there is another sense in which the choice between partiality and generality can be resolved geographically in some instances. Whether partial treatment is adequate is a matter of the connections between the elements of the economy under scrutiny, which is to some degree a matter of geography. The spreading ripples of a change in prices, demands or supplies in one place may dampen to insignificance within a very narrow ambit. If this is the case, then a partial, cost-benefit approach is sufficient since the rest of the economy is virtually unchanged by the disturbance, intervention or investment under investigation. The spread of economic changes was discussed in Chapter 6 in the context of transport network investment.

In making this kind of limited, cost-benefit appraisal, a territorial frame must be deliberated at the outset. It is quite possible that an improvement in welfare for people in one locality may merely signify a transfer from people in another area with no net gain to society as a whole. The Trans-Pennine Motorway, M62, might have generated income from new production in its immediate vicinity, attracted by a reduction in transport costs. To the local economy this is a gain, supposing we can determine that it would not have been so developed in the absence of the new road. With a wider brief it may become clear that all that has happened is curtailment of intended production elsewhere and its relocation. The benefits reduce to the savings in transport costs. The scope of the accounting done depends on the constituency for whom the analysis is undertaken. In the interests of objectivity, however, it seems clear that the broad scope and potential for more general impact should be closely examined before imposing the assumption of a partial analysis. For more significant issues the object of investing in or regulating the economy is often to change the tracery of prices and adjust an unsatisfactory status quo. In geographical terms this might involve attempts to reduce the gap in incomes of people in different regions or the exploitation of a currently inaccessible resource. In such an event, some attempt at a general appraisal is clearly called for and it must account for changes in well-being by the places in which they occur.

Readings

The clarion call to redress the Anglo-Saxon space-less bias is W. Isard's *Location and space economy*, The M.I.T. Press, Cambridge, Massachusetts, 1956. The nature and achievements of the whole and partial approaches to geographical questions in economics are traced to the mid-1960s in two complementary essays: E. M. Hoover, 'Spatial economics: partial equilibrium approach', and L. Moses, 'Spatial economics: general equilibrium approach', in *Encyclopaedia of the Social Sciences*, Macmillan, New York, 1968, pp. 95–100 and 100–108. The most ambitious effort at generality, somewhat off-putting in its here-comes-everything attempts at synthesis, is W. Isard *et al*, *General theory, social, political economic and regional*, The M.I.T. Press, Cambridge, Massachusetts, 1969.

9. Regional Economic Adjustment

For any locality the level of well-being of the population reflects the balance between their assets and liabilities. Insofar as the area trades goods with other parts of the world and uses mobile factors of production, this balance is not autonomous. Changes in the rest of the world are felt as a range of impulses which elicit different responses over time. The change in the nature of the local response is a matter of the length of time needed for different adjustments to work themselves out and come into play. The time dimension can be divided into short-, medium- and long-term, with the break points reflecting the length needed for the markets and resources involved to achieve fluidity. In the short run, the resource endowment of a region and prices also remain fixed when the economy is perturbed by a change in external circumstances. In the medium run, a change in supply or demand conditions in one region will work itself out as changes in prices and quantities traded between regions. A change in the constellation of prices between parts of a nation or the world will have an effect on the relative worth of factors of production and resources. Mineral, climatic and soil resources cannot be moved; however, the encouragement for their discovery, exploitation, technical enhancement, depletion or ruin does vary through time and such changes do affect regional productivity. In combination, variations in regional productivity and factor returns give rise to a long-run response on the part of mobile factors of production. Labour has a greater potential mobility and the migration of people and their talents has been of enormous proportions over the last two centuries. The movement of capital in the form of shifts of plant and machinery is not unknown, but infrequent. The phenomenon most often observed is differences in geographical growth. Industries in some localities decline as worn-out or outmoded plants are abandoned because of a shift in locational advantages. New capacity is installed where geographical advantage is expected to prevail. Money for capital formation is probably the least subject to distance friction in its mobility and its price reflects productivity, risk and uncertainty *in situ*, not according to a geographical pattern. If land rent equalizes transport cost differences, then we should see no transport-related, geographical variation in interest rates, only a reflection of ambient riskiness. However, since the application of new methods and products spreads from some innovative centre through space as well as time, then the application of capital to production and, thus, development processes may show evidence of geographical diffusion.

This array of liquidity of response is best treated by examining first a short-run theory of regional income determination, then inter-regional trade, followed by a consideration of labour and capital mobility and, finally, the diffusion of new goods and techniques.

Short-run Theory of Income and Trade

The Multiplier

To motivate an adjustment in the workings of a region's economy in the first place we can postulate an exogenous change in the location of activities, in investment, in demand or government expenditure. The short run is defined as the period in which such an impulse results only in changes in the employment of resources and thus in incomes, rather than in prices. A shock will not call forth changes in wages, rents, dividends, prices, technology, the distribution of income or the resources available in the area immediately. The presumption is that prices, including factor returns, are sticky, so that rather than take a cut in wages or prices, workers or owners would prefer their resources to be unemployed for a brief time.

The equilibrium income (Y) in a region is determined by the balance of the supply and demand for the use of its resources. Income is defined to consist of consumption spending, investment and government spending (E) plus the balance of trade, being the value of exported goods (T) less the value of imports of both production and consumption goods (M).

$$Y \equiv E + T - M \qquad\qquad 1$$

The demand for the resources of the region in fact depends on price, income and tastes. In the time scale here, prices and tastes will remain constant and, therefore, expenditures within the region and expenditures on imports will depend only on the total level of income in the region. The exports of the region, on the other hand, are independent of local income, being dependent on the income of the rest of the world.

Expenditures on consumption goods, capital goods, and by government increase as income increases at a rate we can label the marginal propensity to spend (b). This is the amount of any increase in income expended. There will be some level of expenditure (a) necessary even if income becomes

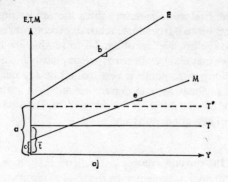

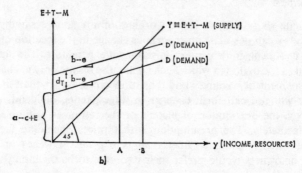

Figure 9.1

zero. Resources will be eaten up to meet these needs and survive. Thus the relationship will be like E in Figure 9.1a and we can express it as:

$$E = a + b\,Y. \qquad\qquad 2$$

Imports will vary similarly, governed by a different constant (c) and by the marginal propensity to import (e).

$$M = c + e\,Y \qquad\qquad 3$$

The level of exports does not vary with regional income but is given from outside as a constant quantity:

$$T = \bar{t}. \qquad\qquad 4$$

The total demands placed on a region's resources are given by the sum of expenditures plus exports less imports, which we can show in Figure 9.1b as the consolidated demand curve D, which will have a slope of $b-e$.

The algebraic equivalent to this diagrammatic manipulation is achieved by substituting 2, 3, and 4 into the original accounting identity of 1 thus:

$$Y = \frac{a-c+l}{1-(b-e)}. \qquad\qquad 5$$

The supply curve for resources is given by the line representing identity 1. Since prices and wages are constant, income and resource use are equivalent. The higher the income, the more resources are being used. Income will fall if labour and capital are unemployed and not getting wages and dividends. The forty-five degree line in figure 9.1b, then, depicts the level of wages and dividends generated by the level of resource employment.

The equilibrium level of income in a region will be where the supply and demand for resources is equal at A. The forty-five degree line represents attainable levels of income and D represents desired levels. The departures between these are reflected in the levels of stocks which sellers maintain. If income is below A, desired expenditures exceed income and stocks are depleting. This induces an increase in production, picking employment and income up towards A. If income were above A, then desired expenditures would be below actual levels and stocks would begin to build up, inducing a reduction in production, employment and income towards the point of balance at A.

The effect of an externally determined change can now be traced and quantified. Let us introduce the change as an increase in demand for the region's exports. Suppose the region in question is South Wales in the 1870s and the world demand for bunker coal for steamships has suddenly burgeoned. This can be represented in figure 9.1a as an upward shift of the exports constant to T'. In total expenditure terms, this shifts the demand for the region's resources in figure 9.1b up to D', an upward parallel shift by dT retaining the same slope $(b-e)$. The demand for and supply of the region's resources will now equate at a higher income level B. The process by which income is raised is as follows. The payments for the increase in coal exports will raise employment of men and capital and thus the earnings of miners and mine owners by dT. This increase will be shared among wages, interest and profits earned by local households (supposing the coal-owners live locally). Some part of the income increase will be spent on goods and services. This is given by $\frac{dE}{dY} = b$, the marginal propensity to spend. Part of these expenditures will be payments to local providers of goods and services, while another part will go for goods imported into the region, this being given by e, the marginal propensity to import. To get the income generated within the region we have to subtract this proportion which goes to buy imports. The net effect, which we can entitle the marginal propensity to spend locally, is given by $b-e = s$.

The local purchases of the miners' and mine-owners' households result in an increase in the income of the providers of goods and services. Some part of this income increase will again be spent on local and imported purchases, increasing local expenditures by the same proportion s. The diminishing rounds of increased expenditure continue in a convergent series:

$$dT + s\, dT + s^2\, dT + s^3\, dT + \ldots \infty.$$

The sum of such a series is equal to

$$\frac{1}{1-s}\, dT$$

where the first term $\dfrac{1}{1-s}$ is called the multiplier. If 60 per cent of any income increase is spent and 40 per cent is spent on imports, then the proportion spent locally would be 20 per cent, i.e. $b-e = s$, $0\cdot6-0\cdot4 = 0\cdot2$. Suppose coal exports were increased by £100,000. The coal-owners' and miners' incomes would increase by £100,000. They would spend £60,000 of this, £40,000 going to buy food, pots and pans, etc. from outside the region. The £20,000 spent locally would raise the incomes of shopkeepers, farmers and manufacturing employers and employees by that amount. They in their turn would spend £4,000 $(0\cdot2^2 \times 100,000)$ on locally produced goods and services. In the next round this would dwindle to £800 $(0\cdot2^3 \times 100,000)$. The sum of these dwindling rounds of effects would approach £125,000, i.e.

$$\frac{1}{1-0\cdot2} \times 100,000 = 1\cdot25 \times 100\cdot000 = £125,000.$$

An increase in coal exports of a given level will raise the income of the population of the region 1·25 times that increase. This multiplier obviously works in reverse so that a decrease in exports of £100,000 will cause a £125,000 drop in income.

The multiplier is the change in income resulting from a change in exports, thus, it is the derivative of Y with respect to T

$$\frac{dY}{dT} = \frac{1}{1-s} \text{ or } dY = \frac{1}{1-s}\, dT.$$

Seen in this fashion it is clear that other types of exogenous change can have the same multiplier effect on income. A change in the level of consumption or imports, causing a parallel shift in the D curve, will have the same effect as a change in imports for

$$\frac{dY}{da} = \frac{1}{1-s} \text{ and } \frac{dY}{dc} = -\frac{1}{1-s}.$$

In the last case, however, the multiplier has a negative sign, since changes in imports have a reverse effect on local income. An increase in imports will reduce local income.

This once-off, isolated picture of a regional economy does underestimate the potential increase in income. The imports generated by increased income will increase the incomes of people in other regions, which will increase their demand for the exports of our original region causing a further increase in income. Suppose these are just two regions with similar propensities to spend and import and isolated from the rest of the world in that the exports of one region equal the imports of the other and vice-versa so that:

$$Y_1 = E_1 + T_{12} - T_{21}$$
$$Y_2 = E_2 + T_{21} - T_{12}.$$

In such circumstances, it is clear that the total multiplier effect of an exogenous increase in investment in region 1, for example, will be $\frac{1}{1-b}$, since there is no import leakage of income increases to the rest of the world. This is obviously a larger effect than that produced by the single-region multiplier.

To be realistic it would be necessary to allow for differing propensities in a larger number of regions than two, with the prospect of an overall balance of trade deficit or surplus with the rest of the world. Such a structure, though cumbersome, can be constructed and does provide a mechanism to explain the transmission of cycles of activity geographically. This is especially true if we break expenditure out into consumption, investment and government outlays.

The Economic Base Multiplier

Data on propensities to spend and import and, indeed, on levels of expenditure and income by region are seldom available. In most countries the only statistics readily available are of regional employment by some standard industrial classification. We have previously referred to a notion of 'basic' export producing employment (B) as opposed to employment geared to providing for the needs of this exporting sector, which we might entitle 'non-basic' (N). If the employed population of a region (T) can be divided into basic and non-basic sectors without too great a degree of arbitrariness, then it is possible to approximate the multiplier. Under the assumption that income is proportional to employment, the proportion of income spent locally is approximated by:

$$s = \frac{N}{T}$$

thus, the multiplier:

$$\frac{1}{1-s} = \frac{1}{1-\dfrac{N}{T}}$$

since $T = N + B$

then $\dfrac{1}{1-s} = \dfrac{T}{B}$.

If the effect of a change on the level of basic, exporting employment can be predicted, then multiplication by the ratio of total to basic employment will give a forecast of total employment and, thus, income. If we know the number of miners employed in producing £100,000 worth of coal, and have observed the ratio of basic to non-basic employees and are confident that it will not change, then we can estimate the total employment effect of an increase in coal exports.

The Input-Output Model

Both the multiplier and its empirical derivative, the economic base ratio, lump activity into the aggregates, expenditure and balance of trade. According to the theory, the income of a region will remain unchanged as long as these quantities remain unchanged. A change in their internal composition will not affect income. If the particular change we wished to predict the result of was a diversion of demand in a region from public transport to cars with no change in aggregate consumption, then the regional income would remain the same. It can be argued that such a change in the composition of demand does disturb the equilibrium. If labour productivity in terms of output per worker is greater in the car-manufacturing business than in the provision of public transport, then the same level of expenditure can be met with fewer workers. This will reduce wage income and consumption and thus regional income. The multiplier cannot account for such changes. To do this, it is necessary to decompose expenditure and production into finer categories so that we may trace such effects. This can be achieved by making some simplifying assumptions about the nature of production relationships in the economy and structuring it as a set of simultaneous linear equations in what is known as input–output analysis.

The elements of production and consumption in a regional economy are related by the physical flows of goods output by one industry which either become inputs to another industry's production process or are finally consumed by households. For example, parts of the output of the steel, glass and rubber industries become inputs to car manufacturing as well as serving consumer needs directly. To simplify matters we will assume that the subsistence needs of a regional economy are met without market transactions and that the only commercially active sectors are a coal-mining industry and an iron industry. The coal industry uses twenty tons a day of its own production to power winding gear and machinery, sends twenty tons to the iron industry and sixty tons to households in the region for domestic heating. This aggregates to a gross output of 100 tons a day. Twenty billets of the iron industry's output become an input of the coal industry to meet the daily need for tools, nails and rails, while fifty billets are used for similar purposes in the iron industry itself and as recycled scrap. Households' needs for agricultural implements, nails, stoves, hollow-ware, etc. are met by an output of thirty billets a day. This gives a gross output of 100 billets. These daily flows of coal and iron can be accounted for in a matrix of flows, as in figure 9.2.

OUTPUT FROM \ OUTPUT TO	COAL	IRON	FINAL DEMAND	GROSS OUTPUT	
COAL	20	20	60	100	TONS
IRON	20	50	30	100	BILLETS

Figure 9.2

These flows are in physical units of production which are only summable across the rows. Flowing in the opposite direction to these are the streams of cash paying for these goods. If we assume that prices in the economy are given, then we can standardize the relationships between sectors by replacing physical flows by their cash counterparts. If 1 ton of coal is priced at £1 and 1 billet of iron is worth 50p, then the cash flows are as in figure 9.3. We can add a row vector to this matrix, to show the inputs from

INPUT TO OUTPUT FROM	COAL	IRON	FINAL DEMAND	GROSS OUTPUT
COAL	20	20	60	100
IRON	10	25	15	50
LABOUR	40	50	10	100
TOTAL INPUT	70	90	85	250

ALL FLOWS IN £

Figure 9.3

outside the complex of inter-industry relations, inputs of labour, capital and land. For simplicity we will label this labour and price it at, say £2 per man day. This set of accounts can be enhanced and elaborated by adding row and column vectors for taxes and government services, imports and exports and other elements of regional accounts. For present purposes we will limit these to final demand and labour inputs.

Taking the inter-industry part of the transactions matrix and dividing the entries in each column by the gross output of the corresponding sector, we obtain a matrix of coefficients which tells us the amount of an input good needed directly to produce one unit of the output of that industry. This matrix of input–output coefficients we signify by A:

$$A = \begin{bmatrix} 20/100 & 20/50 \\ 10/100 & 25/50 \end{bmatrix} = \begin{bmatrix} .2 & .4 \\ .1 & .5 \end{bmatrix}.$$

The other elements of the accounts can be designated as a vector of final demand (D) and of gross output (X):

$$D = \begin{bmatrix} 60 \\ 15 \end{bmatrix} X = \begin{bmatrix} 100 \\ 50 \end{bmatrix}.$$

The workings of the region's economy can now be described as consisting of the amount of inter-industry transactions, i.e. gross output multiplied by the matrix of input–output coefficients, *plus* final demand:

$$X = AX + D.$$

We now wish to solve this set of simultaneous equations for output levels, given the coefficients and final demand. Let us do this algebraically first and then consider what the manipulations mean in terms of the working of the economy.

Faced with an expression $x = ax+d$ in ordinary algebra and wishing to solve it by getting the unknown x on one side of the equations with the known a and d on the other, we would first bring the x values to one side by multiplying both sides by $1-a$, replacing x by $(ax+d)$ on the right-hand side:

$$(1-a)\, x = d.$$

Then we would divide through by $1-a$, to leave:

$$x = \frac{1}{(1-a)}\, d.$$

Similarly, in matrix algebra we multiply through by $(I-A)$, where I is an identity matrix, the equivalent of unity, to get

$$(I-A)\, X = D$$

and then multiply both sides by the inverse of $(I-A)$. By definition a matrix multiplied by its inverse yields an identity matrix leaving:

$$X = (I-A)^{-1}\, D.$$

With this expression we can find equilibrium output levels for any specified vector of final demand. Perturbations from outside the system can be expressed as changes in the final demand vector. The inverse coefficient matrix of the equation traces through the complex of inter-industry relations all the direct and indirect effects on the output of various industries of any change in final demand. For example, an increase in demand for coal of £1 will require 20p of coal and 10p worth of iron to produce. This 20p worth of coal will required 4p worth of coal and 2p worth of iron, while 10p worth of iron requires 4p worth of coal and 5p worth of iron. These effects will continue to spread out through the economy as shown in figure 9.4. These diminishing rounds of effects will aggregate to give the coefficients of the inverted matrix so that £1 increase in coal will require directly and indirectly £1·387 worth of coal and £0·278 worth of iron. In the same way £1 worth of iron will call forth an output of £1·111 worth of coal and £2·222 worth of iron itself. The inverse is the sum of the convergent series at the bottom of figure 9.4. The inverse can be approximated by summing the series up to some power of A for which the elements become insignificantly small. The elements of this inverse matrix indicate

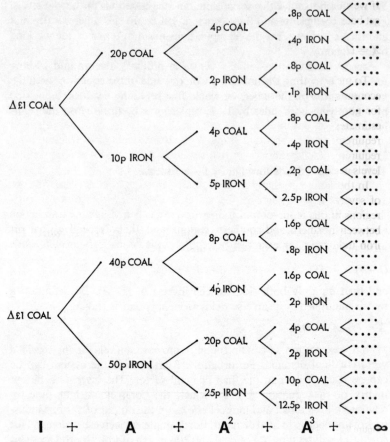

Figure 9.4

the total output required per unit of final demand and the series explains the composition of this total. The first term I accounts for the one unit of output to be delivered to final demand. The second term, A, indicates the direct input required to produce this one unit of final demand. A^2 shows the first-round indirect inputs required to produce A. A^3 shows the second round inputs required to produce A^2, and so on.

In our example, the inverse is:

$$(I-A)^{-1} = \left[\begin{pmatrix} 1 & 0 \\ 0 & 1 \end{pmatrix} - \begin{pmatrix} .2 & .4 \\ .1 & .5 \end{pmatrix} \right]^{-1} = \begin{bmatrix} 1{\cdot}387 & 1{\cdot}111 \\ {\cdot}278 & 2{\cdot}222 \end{bmatrix}.$$

If we take this matrix and multiply the vector of final demand by it, we get back to gross output levels:

$$X = (I-A)^{-1}D = \begin{bmatrix} 1\cdot387 & 1\cdot111 \\ \cdot278 & 2\cdot222 \end{bmatrix} \begin{bmatrix} 60 \\ 15 \end{bmatrix} = \begin{bmatrix} 100 \\ 50 \end{bmatrix}.$$

To measure the impact of some change in circumstances on the regional economy with this formulation, the change is translated into final demand for goods and multiplied by the inverted coefficient matrix. This yields estimates of output levels by sector, taking both direct and indirect requirements into account. Production levels can then be translated into requirements for labour and capital, thus employment and investment levels necessary to meet these final demands.

In the same way that we hinted at stringing the multiplier relationships of several regions together we can treat of the relationships of several regions in this input–output framework. We can envisage the transactions between northern and southern regions and their respective coal and iron industries, for example, presenting a matrix as in figure 9.5. Given

OUTPUT TO / INPUT FROM	NORTH		SOUTH	
	COAL	IRON	COAL	IRON
NORTH COAL	T_{CC}^{NN}	T_{CI}^{NN}	T_{CC}^{NS}	T_{CI}^{NS}
NORTH IRON	T_{IC}^{NN}	T_{II}^{NN}	T_{IC}^{NS}	T_{II}^{NS}
SOUTH COAL	T_{CC}^{SN}	T_{CI}^{SN}	T_{CC}^{SS}	T_{CI}^{SS}
SOUTH IRON	T_{IC}^{SN}	T_{II}^{SN}	T_{IC}^{SS}	T_{II}^{SS}

Figure 9.5

values for these transactions, some of which would be zero, we could in the same way as above establish a set of input–output coefficients, referring not only to inter-industry but also to inter-regional flows. Inverting this matrix it would be possible to quantify, for example, the inputs, direct and indirect, from coal in the South required to produce one unit of iron in the North, thus tracing through industries and regions the effects of a change in economic behaviour.

Shortcomings of the Short-run Models

Both the multiplier theory and input–output analysis are based on an assumption of fixed prices and wages, among other things. If prices are in fact volatile then the results predicted by these models need not be realized. The input–output model is an improvement over the multiplier model, insofar as it allows for changes due to variations in productivity between industries. However, there are many limitations besetting both as representations of the way the economy works.

The multiplier model of regional income determination only applies to a time period over which prices, wages, population, technology and tastes do not change. In the case of prices at least, that can be a very short time indeed. It might be an appropriate vehicle to analyse business cycle impacts: but for perturbations which take a year or more to work out, it is clearly inappropriate. This also holds for the input–output analysis, which assumes fixed prices of goods and factors for its operation.

Even if appropriate in terms of the time horizon, the multiplier model is difficult to implement because data on income, import and export levels, never mind the propensity parameters, are hard to come by. The economic base approximation to the multiplier overcomes this difficulty, but at a cost. It requires the additional assumption that income is proportional to employment. The fact is that different occupations get different wages and an increase in exports from a high-wage industry will have greater secondary effects than expansion in a low-wage industry. Using employment as a proxy also ignores the possibility of increasing productivity with scale and income from land and capital, which in some regions may be large. It also implies that the marginal propensity to spend is equal to the average propensity and will not change with different levels of income. (Although for simplicity the curves in figures 9.1a and b were shown as straight lines, the analysis would in fact hold for any function that could be differentiated.) There is reason to believe that the marginal propensity to spend locally does increase as population increases. As the market expands it gets over thresholds which allow local production of goods formerly imported because the local market was too small. California's growth in the 1920s, 30s, and 40s, based on oil, planes, films, fruit and salad, brought it over the threshold for car assembly, tyre manufacture and even steel production.

In empirical terms the method depends on teasing the employed population out into a basic sector, producing goods for export, and a non-basic sector, producing goods solely for local consumption. This must always be an arbitrary procedure, unless the regions in question are minute. Lumping service and retail employment into the non-basic sector for Cardiff or Edinburgh, never mind London, New York or Chicago, is nonsense.

The input–output method shares some of the debilitating assumptions of the multiplier model, like fixed prices, and has some of its own to boot. In order to represent the economy as a set of linear simultaneous equations, certain restrictions are imposed on the nature of production relationships. In order to treat the relationships between inputs of materials and factors as a number – a fixed coefficient – it must be assumed that the proportions of factors and materials used in the production process are fixed no matter the level of production. No substitution between labour, capital and various materials is permitted. A somewhat lame justification is sometimes offered in terms of the 'current best practice' combination of the industry in question being represented by the coefficient. What the assumption implies is that if output of a good doubles, the use of each of the inputs which go into its production will also double in quantity.

The fixed coefficients used to describe production also deny the possibility of the increasing or decreasing returns to scale implied by the economists' beloved U-shaped average cost curve. This shape implies that inputs do not vary in direct proportion to output. There is some evidence to suggest that for many forms of production, the average cost does not change with scale over a wide range of output levels. The kind of average cost curve used in our analysis of location in Chapter 2, as well as in input–output analysis, is not too grievous a departure from reality.

Using a set of fixed trade coefficients derived from observations of trade flows at one point of time is a more grievous fault. We know trade patterns to be quite volatile and responsive to price changes over time.

When we consider the application of this model to understanding and predicting the workings of regional economies it should be remembered that it was devised with a large, relatively closed economy, that is the U.S.A., in mind. The method treats the technical relationships between the economy's parts as the model's driving force. The smaller the area to which it is applied, the less closed its economy is likely to be and, thus, the more important are trade relationships rather than the model's internal technological configuration in determining the path its economy follows. The level of leakage across its border is largely a matter of size. The world economy contains all its transactions; for the U.S.A. 10 per cent of income is involved in trade; for the U.K. the figure is 40 per cent, while city regions of a country mostly have a higher proportion. The larger the proportion of resources involved in trade, the more resource use will be governed by such relationships. It is, therefore, doubtful if the input–output structure can validly be applied to a small area.

Another issue related to the size of the economy, treated in this fashion, concerns the stability of the coefficients employed. To assume that the technological coefficients will not change rapidly and radically is not too bad for a very large agglomeration of plants in a territory. In such circumstances the behaviour of many plants in one industry in the aggregate might reasonably be represented by a simple common measure, a vector of input–output coefficients. For a small area with a few plants in any one industry, the reality is likely to be more unstable. If the region in question has one coal-burning power plant and a call for increased output is met by building a new oil-burning plant, then the pattern of inputs and outputs in the region is completely changed.

Finally, there is the practical question of collecting data to estimate the coefficients. It is hard enough establishing sales and flows between industries for a national matrix. It becomes an order of magnitude more difficult if the geographical as well as sectoral origins and destinations of transactions have to be accounted for. Data on inter-regional trade are not collected for any regular, administrative purpose, either by firms or government. An inter-regional input–output model usually implies the estimation of inter-regional trade by means of another set of fragile assumptions. These usually involve postulating stable trading arrangements with trade insensitive to changes in either demand or supply circumstances. The suspension of the pricing mechanism, which short-run theories imply, might be reasonable when we consider factors with contractual prices. They make little sense when we consider commodities bought and sold on the closest approximations to perfect markets that exist. Our next step, then, must be to examine the determination of prices and quantities of goods traded between regions, rather than accepting them as given data.

Prices of Goods and Trade Between Regions

We have already put forward a theory of trade between regions when we discussed the demand for transport. Trade occurs between parts of a country or, indeed, between countries, because a price difference exists which is greater than the cost of getting the good from the lower-price to the higher-price area. That provides an incentive to profit-maximizing shippers to buy, ship and sell. Given a large number of these arbitragists, buying from many sellers and selling to many buyers between several places, the final outcome will be a set of trade flows such that the sum of exports equals the sum of imports and a set of prices such that the price in each importing region equals the price in each region that exports to it, plus the unit transport cost between them. This equilibrium can be shown to agree with the maximum value of consumer surplus for the traded good in all the regions. The competitive equilibrium is a socially optimal configuration.

Picking up the two-region case we examined in Chapter 2, suppose we are given the costs of transport between the two regions c_{12} and c_{21} and the prices which equate local supply and demand without trade p_1 and p_2. The final equilibrium is in terms of prices after trade u_1 and u_2 and the volume of trade T_{12} or T_{21}. If $p_2 - p_1 < c_{12}$, there will be no trade. On the other hand, if $p_1 > p_2$ and $p_1 - p_2 > c_{21}$, supplies will flow from 2 to 1, whereas, if $p_1 - p_2 < c_{21}$, again there will be no trade. Thus, if prices differ by less than transport costs, there will be no trade and the final prices will be $u_1 = p_1$ and $u_2 = p_2$. If the gap between the locally determined prices is greater than transport costs, trade will flow from the low-price to the high-price market, as long as the price difference more than covers transport charges. In equilibrium, if p_2 exceeds p_1 by more than c_{12}, then the exports of 1 will equal the imports of Region 2:

$$T_{12} = -T_{21}$$

and the final price in Region 1 will be greater than the original price, while that in Region 2 will be less and they will be related by:

$$u_2 = u_1 + c_{12}.$$

Trade, thus, leads to the geographical convergence of prices, with the cost of transport maintaining whatever gradient there is. In the absence of costs of distance friction, prices would everywhere be the same.

It becomes computationally cumbersome to extend this analysis full-blown to treat relationships between many regions. If we simplify the situation by assuming that there are fixed quantities to be traded, however, it can be managed quite easily. Consider, for example, an Indonesian island where rice is the staple and every household consumes a similar amount. Geographical variations in soil fertility, terrain, water available and population density result in differences in rice output per capita. If we divide the island into a number of regions $(1, 2 \ldots, i, j, n)$ with fixed production S_i and consumption D_i, then we can calculate the surpluses in regions where production exceeds consumption

$$S_i - D_i = T_i$$

and the deficits in areas where consumption is greater than production

$$D_j - S_j = T_j.$$

We will assume that the island is just self-sufficient so that surpluses and deficits net out to zero

i.e. $\sum_i T_i = \sum_j T_j.$

(This is not an essential requirement and the analysis can be carried out in terms of inequalities with some slack allowing for net exports or net imports from abroad. For present purposes the equality avoids confusion.) Knowing the unit cost of transporting rice from each region with a surplus to each deficit region, c_{ij}, the problem is to determine which deficits to serve from which surpluses in the most efficient fashion. Efficiency in this case is a matter of reducing the transport bill involved to a minimum. This objective we can write as a desire to minimize:

$$C = \sum_i \sum_j T_{ij} \, c_{ij}. \qquad 6$$

This problem is solved by selecting the right inter-regional flows T_{ij}. These must be such that the requirements of each deficit area are just met:

$$\sum_i T_{ij} = T_j \qquad 7$$

and that the surpluses of the other regions are just exhausted:

$$\sum_j T_{ij} = T_i. \qquad 8$$

To avoid a confusion of signs, we are dealing only in positive flows in the exporting direction and, thus, constrain the solution values so that they are non-negative:

$$T_{ij} \geq 0. \qquad 9$$

Mathematically, finding the solution of this problem involves minimizing the linear objective function subject to the linear constraints. It constitutes a classical application of linear programming – the Transportation Problem.

It is characteristic of linear programmes that the solution of a minimization problem automatically yields the solution to its maximizing dual. This negative image of the primal problem involves in this case maximizing:

$$Z = \sum_j u_j T_j - \sum_i u_i T_i. \qquad 10$$

This is clearly what shippers are seeking to do, to maximize the difference between their receipts from sales in deficit areas and payment for supplies in surplus areas. Given the large number of shippers competing with each other, this search for profits will result in a final set of equilibrium prices governed by the limiting relationship:

$$u_j - u_i = c_{ij}. \qquad 11$$

In competition they will continue to buy ships and trade to the point where the price gap just equals transport costs and surplus profits are zero.

Perfect competition, as replicated by the mathematics of optimization, prevents any curtailment of trade and creation of profit.

The method of solving this Transportation Problem can be found in any standard operations research book. Broadly, the search for a best solution is started by finding any feasible solution to the problem, that is one which satisfies the constraints 7, 8, and 9. The price limit of the dual 11 is then used to establish 'shadow' prices at origins and destinations implied by this initial solution. For all the pairs of surplus and deficit areas not joined in the feasible solution an opportunity cost, forgone in not sending a unit of the good between the relevant source and destination, can be calculated as the difference between their shadow prices. A procedure is then followed to shift some traffic from the initial allocation towards the pairs of regions where the difference between the opportunity cost and the transport cost is greatest. In this, care is taken to maintain the satisfaction of the constraints on requirements and availabilities 7 and 8. This process is repeated from the stage of calculating shadow prices until all the opportunity costs are less than or equal to their corresponding transport costs. This finally satisfies the constraint of the dual 11, and indicates the achievement of a position which cannot be bettered.

This formulation of the trade problem provides another link between land use and transport costs. The shadow prices u_i and u_j can be conceived of as measures of comparative cost advantage. If we discount all possible geographical variables other than transport costs, assuming equal resource endowment and costs in regions, then the dual values of this problem represent measures of the advantage accruing to places in terms of production and consumption by dint of their location. Stevens (1961), in treating these relationships, quotes Marshall's 'Principles of Economics':

If two producers have equal facilities in all respects except that one has a more convenient situation than the other and can buy or sell in the same markets with less cost of carriage, his differential advantage ... is the aggregate of the excess charges for cost of carriage to which his rival is put ... this becomes the situation value of his site.

'Situation' value is the same as 'location' rent in the sense in which we used it in Chapter 2.

Long-run Adjustments

Regional Supply and Demand Differences

Trade in goods is the shorter-run equilibriating process which operates to smooth out differences in supply and demand conditions in various parts of a country, or the world. The differences between the coincidence of local supply and demand which generates trade arise because supply conditions and demand conditions vary geographically. Production costs vary because of differences in the dower of climate, soil and minerals, and because of variations in the quantity and quality of capital and labour available. The quantities demanded at various prices differ from place to place with real disposable incomes, tastes and traditions.

If we consider all factors of production to be immobile, then we would expect the process of inter-regional trade we have just described to tend to equalize not only commodity prices between regions, but also wages, rents, dividends and rates of return on capital between regions. The exploitation of comparative cost advantages and specialization in production according to resource and factor availability will substitute trade for factor mobility and narrow regional differentials in returns. A region with plentiful labour and little capital will specialize in and export labour-intensive products requiring much labour and little capital. It will import goods requiring a large capital input from regions with costly labour and cheap capital. Inter-regional trade will, however, fail to eradicate differences in returns completely. The persistence of real income differences, rates of return on capital and rewards to enterprise excites a longer-term adjustment process consisting of the migration of labour, managerial skill and differences in capital formation between parts of the world along with the diffusion of technical innovations from where they were first applied to the rest of the economy. Mobile factors of production will move from where the returns to their employment are lower to where they are higher, thus narrowing the geographical differentials in wages, interest and profit.

In addition to physical resources of the land and climate, there is one other factor which affects comparative advantage which cannot migrate. This is location itself. The advantage accruing to favourable position vis-à-vis other activities and markets, largely accruing in terms of transport costs, cannot be eradicated. Some geographical differences in prices and returns will persist because of variations in land, mineral and climatic wealth, but also because we do not live in a one-point world and superior location is a very real advantage. Technological advances in transport which reduce the friction of distance, in effect shrinking the globe, reduce the potency of this advantage and the income differences which arise because of it. But, unless we achieve instantaneous, costless transport, some places will be advantaged by their greater accessibility. Such was the advantage of Rome at the heart of the middle sea: Paris at the centre of its basin: the Ruhr at the junction of the Börde and the Rhine: London at the nexus of sea routes and Lowland Britain: New York providing a gateway to the interior and Chicago at the focus of the Midwest.

Labour Migration

As a starting point for a discussion of the movement of labour let us postulate a perfectly competitive economy in which resources, capital and technology are fixed and in which there is perfect knowledge of opportunities. There are no costs of migration. Labour is homogeneous and workers act so as to maximize real wages. The best distribution of population in a nation will be that which achieves the greatest real income per head in each locality. (Real income is cash income adjusted for cost-of-living differences.) Under perfect competition, this will also maximize national income per head. The level of income per head in a region will depend on the balance between scale economies and diminishing returns to scale. We can represent the relationship of output or income per head and regional population by the average product curve in figure 9.6. As

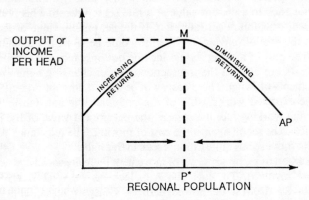

Figure 9.6

population increases towards P^*, productivity per capita will increase as a greater local market allows specialization and scale economies to be enjoyed. After a peak of productivity per head at P^*, diminishing returns set in with congestion and crowding clogging the use of the limited resource base. National income per head will be greatest if population moves between regions until wages everywhere equal the marginal product of labour, a position upon which no one can improve by changing their location. Given a perfectly competitive labour market, employers will hire up to the point where the product of hiring the last man is just equal to his wage.

This theory would predict that if there are real wage differences between places, then labour will migrate from low-wage to high-wage regions until wages are equalized. In reality labour markets are far from competitive, being better characterized as monopolist, monopsonist games. The predilection of national unions for national wage rates does tend to blur the issue. In addition migration is a costly business and the benefits involved do have a time horizon. Harking back to Chapter 6 and our statement of the investment decision rule, we might state the individual's migration calculation as follows:

$$\text{if } c_{ij} < \frac{(w_{j1}-w_{i1})}{(1+r)} + \frac{(w_{j2}-w_{i2})}{(1+r)^2} + \ldots + \frac{(w_{jn}-w_{in})}{(1+r)^n}$$

then migrate from i to j. He must consider the difference in wages between where he is now (w_i) and some alternative place and employment (w_j), over his expected working life (n years), discounting the future income difference back to a present value at a rate (r) representing his preference for present over future consumption. If the net present value of the move exceeds the cost of moving, c_{ij}, then it would be worthwhile making the move. The cost of moving should include not only removal expenses and travel costs but also all the transaction costs of changing homes and the arrangements of living. These costs will be a fixed amount no matter how long the expected working life of the potential migrant. Obviously the shorter the working life, the smaller the net present value of the income difference to be set off against the cost of moving. The reluctance of older people to move seems quite rational seen in this light.

In addition to pecuniary costs of movement there are social and aesthetic wrenches involved. To leave the Appalachians or West Kerry or the Hebrides for Detroit or Birmingham or Glasgow hurts. That this is balanced against income opportunities finds expression in sayings about scenery and filling your stomach, as well as in the annual pilgrimage back to the highlands and islands. There are opposite forces of revulsion at work elsewhere, which exceed mere wages in their potency. Amongst blacks in the U.S.A., agricultural labour in the South is not far enough removed from slavery, even if it paid well. Social advantages attach to destinations in addition to wage differences. The big city offers an urban density of your own kind, entertainment and intercourse which the country does not afford. Indeed, it offers the opportunity to choose a different kind and type of life, to some.

Even if knowledge of wage differences is readily available, making a discount for natural emigrants' boastfulness, knowledge of cost of living differences is seldom complete. In addition, labour is far from homogeneous and besides questions of matching skills there are questions of satisfaction. Coal-face workers might well consider working in a brassière factory demeaning and country boys might hate being inside at all. An extremely potent force in migration is that of tradition – even if of very recent origin. On the face of it some groups have an overdeveloped propensity to shift, even if the economic motive to migrate has dwindled in significance. There is still a curiosity about the land beyond the horizon. The readiness with which Americans up stakes and move reflects this, when it is compared with the clinging to locality and home of Great Britain. Looking at recent changes in U.S. population it appears that the push of big city life in the North-East and Midwest is being matched by the pull of the warmer open spaces of the South, Texas, New Mexico, Arizona, Colorado, and Oklahoma. Although many of the differences might be expressed as matters of cost of living, there is a degree to which that would fail to capture the life-style questions involved. There are signs of growing stability in the U.S.A., which may be taken as indicative of maturity or degeneration. Whatever its long-term effects, this slowing down of the percentage of movers from 19·1 per cent of the population in 1970 to 17·7 per cent in 1978 seems to result from greater emphasis on amenities than cash in preference orderings.

If we relax the static structure of the theory we started out with and allow of capital investment and technical advance, then the average product curve can shift with changing population. In this case real wage differences along with migration become reflections of the same underlying force, geographical differences in the pace of economic growth. This matter will be taken up in more detail in Chapter 10. For now it suffices to suggest that high-growth areas offer not only higher real wages but also a wider range of opportunities, greater security and continuity of employment. Nevertheless, wage differences remain a powerful force in governing population movements.

Given this complexity of motives and circumstances, it is unlikely that a simple deductive approach to migration will yield a strong explanation. There is thus an inclination to adopt a more inductive mode of inquiry and seek an answer by looking at the actual pattern of movements, trying to identify some variables which coincide with the pattern statistically and which, therefore, might afford an explanation in terms of the relative strength of different influences.

Looking at geographical movements of people in an urbanized society in a period of stability, it does seem that more people leave large towns than small towns, that more go to big towns than smaller ones and that more people move short distances than long distances. Translating these proportionalities into an equality with a constant, these observations produce the familiar form of what has been entitled a gravity model from its resemblance to Newton's second law:

$$M_{ij} = k \frac{P_i P_j}{f(dij)}$$

where M_{ij} = number of people leaving place i to go to place j
P_i, P_j = the populations of $i+j$
$f(dij)$ = some function of distance between i and j
k = a constant of proportionality.

Similar justification can be offered for its application to migration as was put forward for its use in predicting travel in Chapter 5.

Such an expression can be fitted quite well to the seemingly random flicker of movements which characterize a basically stable population distribution. It falls down when applied to sweeping changes such as the colonization of North America of the nineteenth century or the surge to the coalfields of the highland fringe of the British Industrial Revolution. This charge can also be levelled at an alternative formulation which treats distance implicitly by replacing it with a measure of the opportunities for satisfaction of the migrant's needs between his origin and final destination to give:

$$M_{ij} = a \frac{O_j}{O_{ij}}$$

where O_j = number of opportunities at j
O_{ij} = number of intervening opportunities between i and j
a = a constant.

The myth of the Manifest Destiny of the U.S.A., realized in its burgeoning frontier, vastly overwhelmed any careful evaluation of intervening opportunities.

Economic indicators of geographical repulsion and attraction, such as wage and income differences, have been employed to explain migration in the U.S.A. but, since the data referred to the 1950s, a climatic variable had to be added to accommodate the fact that a major movement to California was under way. However, the most important variable in explaining movement in that period was the prior volumes of migrants. This suggests considerable stability in the pattern of migration. If that is the case, an even more inductive approach suggests itself. Why not take some historical contingency table for migration, a matrix of flows from origins to destinations, and assume that the pattern and process displayed is stable through time? The flow matrix, with entries M_{ij}, can be transformed into a transition probability matrix by dividing each element in it by the corresponding row sum, i.e. the total number of migrants originating in any one region so that:

$$\frac{M_{ij}}{\sum_{j} M_{ij}} = P_{ij} \text{ where } \sum_{i} P_{ij} = 1.$$

P_{ij} can be considered as the probability that an individual selected at random from the population of region i will move to region j in the chosen time period. If we multiply a vector of initial population C_{to} by the matrix of P_{ij} values P, we age the population by one migration cycle to the next time period t_1:

$$C_{to} P = C_{t1}.$$

In general, if we multiply the original population by the P matrix powered up, we will achieve forecasts of multiples of the chosen time period:

$$C_{to} P^2 = C_{t2}$$

and in general $C_{to} P^n = C_{tn}$.

A process like this will reach a stationary state, where $C_{tn-1} = C_{tn}$, if P is non-singular, i.e. if it has an inverse. At that juncture successive applications of the transition matrix will result in no change of regional populations, net migration will be zero. The equilibriating characteristics, the length of time the process takes to achieve stability, the effect of the initial distribution of population on this type of probabilistic process, may be explored with the mathematics of Markov chains. The objective of such endeavours is to indicate how populations change and stabilize under assumptions of stationary migratory or demographic behaviour. There is every indication of considerable volatility in how fast we reproduce and where we migrate to. The booms and slumps of birth-rates since the 1920s, the stemming of the drift to the South in England in the late 1960s and to California in the U.S.A., are evidence of this. This revealed volatility suggests that the relevance of this Markovian treatment to the prediction or understanding of migration is not great.

Capital Movement

Investment funds are without a doubt the most geographically liquid of assets. Once planted as buildings and machinery they become the most immobile, whose locational shifts are long-term reflections of the path of economic and technological change. Bankers and lending agents increasingly live in Melvin Webber's 'urban non-place realm', viewing the world in passage, not as if from some fixed point. Their vision of profitability and risk is, hopefully, no longer jaundiced by geographical prejudice, although national prejudice may still operate. The charges for capital funds represent judgements on *in situ* riskiness, which does not necessarily increase with distance from the financial centres in London or New York. It was not always so. For example, Ulysses Simpson Grant's partner, a St Louis real-estate dealer, made a trip to Philadelphia in 1858 to secure some money from financiers there. On the east coast the going rate of interest was 5 per cent, in St Louis it was 10 per cent. He offered the Philadelphians 8 per cent and hoped, vainly, to make a living on the difference. With a fully integrated communication and banking system, financial transactions now cost little and the costs do not vary significantly with distance, so such gradients do not persist. Innately risky environments and activities, such as Great Plains farming or North Sea oil recovery, obviously call for a premium on interest rates.

In effect we examined the major element in the mobility of capital in treating industrial location in Chapter 2. It is largely a matter of siting new factories and infrastructure and the abandonment of antiquated plant and locations. Buildings are virtually immobile, as is much machinery. By the time its location is called into doubt, it is likely to be old and not worth moving. In effect the only opportunity cost of such capital is its scrap value. Production will continue to the point where the present value of the expected stream of earnings exceeds the scrap value of the capital.

Monopoly power can be wielded to protect the returns to deeply sunk capital from the effects of changes in locational fortune. As we remarked earlier, the Pittsburgh Plus pricing scheme, under which the U.S. steel cartel from 1900 to 1924 priced as if all steel delivered came from Pittsburgh, was such an endeavour. With reductions in the coal input required to produce steel, the geographical advantage was swinging from the coalfields to the southern tip of Lake Michigan, at the heart of the Midwest market and on water for the receipt of iron ore, and to the southern end of the Appalachians, with cheap coal, ore and labour. The cartel's hold on prices was finally broken in 1948, with a consequent strengthening of the position of Gary and Birmingham.

The Geographical Spread of Technical Change

If we hold the physical resources of a locality and its labour and capital resources constant, the wealth of its population may still grow because labour and capital are used more efficiently, employing better production and management techniques. Administrative managerial talent can be considered another labour skill subject to similar desires and urges to those we have discussed previously. Entrepreneurial capacity increasingly dwells in the same realm as finance, associated with the headquarters of firms with many plants and products but not tied to a base, and constantly seeking profitable ventures wherever they lie. The railroad baron wandering around North America in his private car provided a prototype for this behaviour.

Technical progress and the development of new products mostly take place in existing agglomerations of industrial and commercial activity, thereby potentially reinforcing those economies which accrue to agglomerations. This reinforcement will not be a strong and lasting force if the innovations can be broadcast geographically with speed and ease. Once proprietary secrecy to gain monopoly profits breaks down, there are two factors which govern the speed of adoption of a new product or process across the land. The first is the means of transmission, the channels of communication both general and specific. The existence of conduits for the circulation of papers and journals, the postal and phone systems, the means of travel, trade associations and presses, agricultural advisory services etc. mean that the additional cost of spreading the word about a new technique is minute. Newspapers and commercial television and radio systems broadcast information about new products while the velocity of circulation of people in the country, governed to some degree by the cost of movement, controls the rate at which information can potentially pass by word of mouth. In an under-developed economy, where these channels are costly or non-existent, the cost of transmission may be enormous, involving building up the network to spread the word from scratch.

The other governing factor is the vulnerability of the receivers, whether they will accept and apply the word. This might be a technical matter, whether they can or cannot, whether it is appropriate to their needs. Or it might be a matter of attitude, whether they are Luddite in inclination or growth-minded.

Insofar as the cost of communication does to a degree vary with distance and the receptiveness of potential adopters to change does vary from place to place, we would expect the spreading process to manifest itself geographically. For both consumer and industrial markets there is evidence of some regularity in the temporal pattern of a product or process. Adopters are normally distributed through time about an average time of adoption. Accumulating adopters over this distribution we end up with an S-shaped curve of market penetration over time as in figure 9.7. Adopters can be characterized by their position in this sequence. The innovators are venturesome, less averse to risk because they are wealthier, having

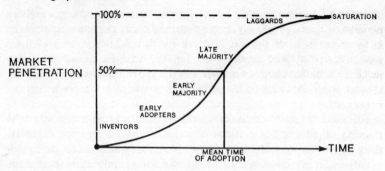

Figure 9.7

larger, more specialized farms or firms or practices than the average. Their orientation is cosmopolitan, identifying with their profession or calling rather than their locality. Their important social contacts are with others who do the same thing. Their major sources of information are technical literature, mass media, other innovators and change agents, such as agricultural advisors or salesmen. They influence the diffusion process by demonstration rather than by personal interaction or social force. People of this kind are likely to be concentrated near the centre of innovation, which will most frequently be the main city of the country. The early stages of spread will percolate down the hierarchy of towns as foci of the communication system.

The early adopters are community opinion leaders bringing social pressure and word-of-mouth communication into the process. They tend to be wealthier, more educated and successful than average and more mobile geographically, occupationally and socially. They have more exposure to mass media and there is a theory that these are the people who are influenced by advertising and then influence others. Their effect on the geography of the process is to begin its spread by a neighbourhood effect, rippling out from the central place foci in wavelike fashion, in addition to the channelized flow of the first stage. This brings the early majority into play, whose characteristic deliberation and thoroughness in decision-making removes any stigma attached to novelty for its own sake, waiting for evidence of success before adopting. The later majority are often less well off, older and sceptical. When they accept the good or technique it has become a necessity and they depend on word-of-mouth and personal experience for information. The laggards in the process are reached as saturation is approached. Geographically, they are often located in the interstices between central places and in the periphery of the nation.

Their social focus is very local, having limited outside contacts. Tradition plays a stronger role in their decision-making than market considerations. In industrial markets, the last adopters are often small firms with limited growth potential. They may be quite profitable with a safe, isolated market niche and uninterested in increasing volume or operating efficiency. Given the massive concentration of industrial activity which we previously noted, and the concentration of scientists, technologists, research establishments and company headquarters that go along with it, it is no surprise that most industrial advance is narrowly confined and that the more far-flung parts of an economy do not exhibit much innovatory behaviour.

With national communication media there is no reason why the diffusion process should not be extremely rapid and the ultimate cause of speed or failure to adopt a matter of receptiveness, not geographical distance from the source. Receptiveness might well vary geographically and it is possible that this reflects a lack of adoption of change in the past, when communications were poorer. But that is an historical explanation, not an economic one.

With this discussion of the spread of products and production techniques we complete a picture of geographical economic adjustment processes and prepare the way for a discussion of how an economy's growth varies over the land.

Readings ·

For this chapter, and indeed the whole book, I have drawn heavily on ideas in:

H. O. Nourse, *Regional Economics*, McGraw-Hill, New York, 1968, and
H. W. Richardson, *Regional Economics*, Praeger, New York, 1969.

A more recent treatment of the same material is E. M. Hoover,
Regional Economics, 2nd edition, Knopf, New York, 1975.

The relationship between rent and transport costs is handled in:
B. H. Stevens, 'Linear programming and location rent', *Journal of Regional Science*, no. 3, 1961, pp. 15–25.

The movement of people is given a sociological treatment in E. S. Lee,
'A theory of migration', *Demography*, no. 3, 1966, pp. 47–57, and a mathematical one in A. Rogers, *Multiregional Mathematical Demography*, Wiley, New York, 1975.

The most complete statement on the spread of cultural and economic change is J. C. Hudson, *Geographical Diffusion Theory*, Northwestern University Studies in Geography, Evanston, Ill., no. 19, 1972.

10. The Geography of Growth

In effect the subject of economic growth was broached when an economic landscape was built up in Chapter 3. It was central to the discussion of agglomeration economies and the last chapter dealt with some of the geographic processes involved in economic adjustment and growth. It is now time to dwell exactly on the combination of circumstances which lead to the expansion of the wealth per person of an economy and which we call economic growth. Most of the theory put forward thus far has attended to the problem of sharing limited resources among various uses in an instantaneous world without technical or attitudinal change among a given population of actors. The process of economic growth is compounded of a multiplicity of political, demographic, technical and preferential events, decisions and discoveries. So far no generalized abstraction has come close to mirroring the richness of the real process. Some of its principal components have, however, been isolated in a fashion which is of use. They provide light in seeking policies to raise well-being in regions and countries where people have not enjoyed much relief from hunger and the limitations of poverty.

One overarching question is that of the physical resources of our world, their extent, exploitation and depletion. There has been much written on this of late and many of the questions raised are matters of geographical fact. However, little of the outpouring could be counted as theory. It is frequently apocalyptic and beyond the ken of political economy, with the merit of a viewpoint determined by the volume of the prophet's voice. The problem of evaluating physical resources is a matter of comparing the utilities of different generations and guessing what technical advance might occur and how tastes will change. For present purposes, the physical resource endowment must be kept in mind as the ultimate limitation on the development process. Given such an upper bound, an explanation of the development process with predictive capability would need several elements. Firstly, the processes of population change and capital formation and their interaction should be articulated. How the views, desires, aptitudes and capacities of the population change over time needs to be understood. Finally, the causes and effects of technological improvement must be accounted for. The last two elements are inherently unpredictable and only amenable to historical explanation in terms of a sequence of unique human purposes and choices with no necessary or sufficient general cause. To venture more absolute causes is an interesting but over-simple speculation. Some quantitative propositions about population change and capital accumulation and their interactions are possible, and provide a prelude and basis for any qualitative conjectures on changes in human resources and technical progress.

Population and Capital

The classical formulation of the growth problem had part of the output of the economy going as wages to maintain labour at a subsistence level. An additional part goes to landowners as rent. This is the difference between the price of a good set by the production costs of the marginal producer and any other producer's production costs. Costs in agriculture rise as output expands. The residuum of total output goes to those who have invested in machinery, as profits. The unit cost of manufacturing with this equipment remains constant with changes in output.

If a capitalist invests in making more machinery, wage payments will be increased to employ labour in this endeavour. This causes population to increase which, in turn, calls for an increase in the output of food. Because agriculture is subject to diminishing returns, the price of food and thus rents will rise. The manufacturer's wage bill increases as more labourers require more expensive subsistence. The cost-determined price of manufactured goods remains constant and so the capitalists' profit dwindles and investment and growth are discouraged. The Malthusian spectre of people outstripping food supply grinds any growth to a halt.

Obviously, improvements in production methods which increase output per head would release this constraint on the process. Allowing that such developments have occurred, then the path of growing wealth traces a balance between increasing investment (and the savings to finance it) and consumption. The motive for increasing productive capacity is to serve increasing consumption. Yet the supply of the means of production must be met by non-consumption of some of the national product. Setting aside government and overseas trade and rearranging the Keynesian aggregates introduced in the last chapter, we can divide calls on the nation's output into demand for consumer goods and for investment goods. The supply of output is determined by the employment of available resources and the level of technology. There is one level of income at which demand for output is just equal to the full employment supply of resources. In order for this full-employment income level to be sustained over time in a steady growth path, both total demand and supply must increase at the same rate. This precarious state arises because investment to get full employment in one time period increases productive capacity and the supply of output in a subsequent period. If excess capacity is to be avoided, demand must increase to consume the increased supply. The rate of capital accumulation must be exactly equal to the rate of population growth. The mathematics of this are shown in the Appendix to this chapter.

The balance of population and national income depends on the amount of equipment needed to produce a given level of output. The value of this *capital/output ratio* for developed countries is of the order of 3:1, when land, physical resources and overseas holdings are excluded from its calculation. At this rate it takes 3 per cent of the national product devoted to new investment to make total income grow 1 per cent per annum. If population is growing more rapidly than this, the increase in income will be more than absorbed by population growth, resulting in static or diminishing income per head, and thus, no growth in the sense usually employed. With population growth much less than 3 per cent, as in Europe, North America and the Soviet Union, growth of 3 per cent per annum in income per person can be achieved by devoting about 10 per cent of income to net investment. This is well within the range which has been customary over the last century or more. A densely underdeveloped country, such as Mexico, with a 3·5 per cent rate of population growth has difficulty in allocating the 5 per cent of any year's output to investment necessary to yield a 1 per cent increase in total income, never mind the 12 per cent required to raise income per person. Spain, which must be counted among the less developed, with slower population growth at 1 per cent per annum, can hold income per capita with a 3 per cent level of investment. Anything over this contributes to rising output per person. What is true for countries obviously holds for different parts of the same country.

Balanced or Unbalanced Growth Versus Comparative Advantage

The setting aside of trade relations, which permits the simple generalization on the rate of capital accumulation and population growth to emerge, also sets aside the classical economic principle of comparative advantage. According to this principle, growth is promoted by trade arising from specialization in production according to the opportunity cost of products in various regions. This generates a conflict in theories about growth and policies prescribed to engender growth. Those who see growth as a matter of changing the relations among producers, consumers and investors, usually consider trade as an external stimulus to be manipulated to encourage technological advance or a change in the economic balance of power in a region. The policies which arise from such a viewpoint may be quite at odds with those which are based on employing resources and factors producing and exporting goods for which the region's producers have a lower opportunity cost and importing those for which the opportunity cost is higher. The opportunity cost of a product is the value of the factors used to produce it in the next best use, i.e. its market price. This strategy of specialization according to market prices might encourage continued dependence on an agricultural surplus and strongly deter the emergence of manufacturing and the urbanization of the population of a region.

Such a specialization trajectory for a regional economy runs contrary to the 'balanced growth' strategy. Under balanced growth, simultaneous expansion of several sectors is deemed desirable since it results in greater return to investment due to dynamic external economies generated by the horizontal and vertical interdependence of many sectors.

There is a contrary view of the dynamics involved which proclaims 'unbalanced growth' more appropriate. This implies a concentration of resources on a leading sector to economize on very sparse entrepreneurial skill. It is held that this vanguard of growth will draw the rest of the economy along in its wake. In geographical terms this has been translated into the notion of concentrated 'poles of growth', defined in terms of access to cheap power, materials, abundant trainable labour or existing transport facilities. The results of applying this theory may also run counter to those arising from the comparative advantage theory. An unbalanced growth path may be more effective because it focuses the limited potential for enterprise in a region or provides a stronger incentive for political action to bring about needed constitutional or institutional change. These criteria have nothing to do with comparative advantage and the selected focus might be altogether different from the activity which enjoys the lowest opportunity costs. Comparative advantage will often point to agriculture or extraction while the dictates of unbalanced dynamics would encourage the development of manufacturing, particularly heavy engineering. This latter was the strategy of the Cassa per il Mezzogiorno from 1957 to 1965, producing the 'cathedrals in the desert' such as the Alfasud car plant near Naples and the unfinished Iri steel works at Gioia Tauro. The construction of this was halted by the slump in the world steel market of the mid-1970s and it stands perhaps as a mute object lesson for those who would ignore comparative cost theory.

Other political and social objectives, greater equality of wealth and opportunity and the tearing down of racial and class barriers, may not be brought about by market forces. They may be incompatible with comparative advantage. As yet, no one has derived a ready way of incorporating these criteria in a theoretical analysis of the working of the economy to produce a simple prescription. The resolution of these problems must be a matter for political skills and remedies.

Duality

Industrialized societies overcame the Malthusian barrier by attaining, despite cyclical setbacks, an investment rate which kept output surging ahead of population. The mobilization of greater productive capacity in developed areas of the world grew in a seed-bed of geographically and occupationally flexible societies which accepted and applied new means of production to an ever-widening range of products. Technical innovation and the exploitation of new resources demand entrepreneurs and workers willing and able to change what, how and where they produce as the need arises. Society must provide a socially and geographically fluid medium to accommodate ceaseless change in the relative worth of occupations and locations as the blend and amounts of goods and services required change through time. In Europe and North America vast sweeps of migration and occupational structure have transformed society over the last two centuries. More viscous communities with strong attachments to place, caste and calling may lead to the retention of older ways. Rigid power structures and inefficient production result in population growth eating up output and choking off capital accumulation.

This social viscosity can vary geographically within a country as well as between world regions and finds expression in economic 'duality'. In many lands the acceptance of new methods does not percolate far beyond a few points of contact with the world of commerce. Within national frontiers two economies may be observed. A back country of traditionally-organized subsistence farmers surrounds limited commercialized areas dependent on foreign trade for markets. The traditional sector may draw succour in aid and charity from the developed sector with little recompense, or it may provide an unrewarded source of tax revenue. Frequently, the dissident affection of its population for the central authority dissipates the national wealth in military adventure and repression. The actual or perceived opportunities of the commercialized sector usually, however, provide a magnet and safety valve for the traditional sector. Whatever the relations between the two sectors, the balance is usually an economically arbitrary one of power, not particularly conducive to material advancement for the entire population.

All nations have some vestiges of this duality. Appalachian hill folk and Bayou Cajuns, the Gaels of the Atlantic fringe of Scotland and Ireland, the Montagnards of Indo-China and the Masai of Kenya all exhibit various degrees of resistance to the assimilation of modernity in production, commerce and way of life. It is noticeable that the resistance of most such groups is stiffened and abetted by the rigours and physique of their homelands and their inaccessibility. Where the modern sector is created by world demand for exports of some primary commodities, development and change are often carried no further. This duality poses most of the 'regional' problems associated with development. Modernized regions may wish to relieve themselves of a burden by encouraging the commercialization of the rest of the country. The envy of the subsistence sector combined with political potency may induce actions to speed the permeation of change via remedies such as agricultural and power schemes, or road or rail building.

Regional Politics

With a high enough rate of saving in an economy, the growth-maximizing allocation of resources between kinds and locations of investment would ideally be found by the workings of a perfectly competitive market. The lean markets for new products where society is only emerging from subsistence are, however, splendid breeding grounds for monopolies. Thus, the desired reflection of incremental costs in prices will not necessarily come about unaided by government. There are in addition nationalistic, utopian, partisan and sectional motives which far outweigh the simple objective of economic efficiency in inciting intervention in pricing and investment decisions. An ideal collective economy, perfect computation, calculating and imposing the marginal conditions for efficiency, could do better than the ideal competitive solution. The distortions of natural monopolies and significant external costs and benefits attached to some forms of production could be remedied. The realities are seldom close to either ideal.

The territorial basis of most forms of representative government is a strong incentive for politicians to vie for short-term equal shares of growth for regions of divergent resources and capacities. The vagaries of political power, the constitution, parties and personalities can lead to geographical dispositions of national wealth quite at odds with the best interests of the whole nation. The Federalist checks and balances of the American Constitution strongly over-represent rural and propertied interests. The tribal loyalties underpinning military power have often imparted a geographical bias to spending. Centrifugal Stalinist regional policy was not unrelated to the Georgian's origins and his power base among non-Russian nationalities, for whom he was once Commissar. Depressed agricultural prices in favour of the proletariat push down the farmer. Soaking up a concentration of unemployment with a big industrial estate may simply draw together what would have developed elsewhere, merely transferring unemployment with no net gain in output. Driving a railway into an area of persistent under-employment may simply create twin streaks of rust across the land, while traffic clogs in less politically sensitive parts of the country. These departures from economic efficiency can hold the economy back from raising output per person most rapidly. Clearly the relations between regional and national objectives need closer scrutiny if the right priorities are to be determined.

City and Umland under Growth

Recalling the simplified geography of Chapter 2 we can envisage an under-developed economy to consist of a central city producing investment goods and manufactures with labour and capital subject to constant average costs. The rural surrounds of this city are partly used for commercial agricultural production. Subsistence producers cannot do more than meet their own needs, for lack of capital. Capital and hired labour can be employed to transform land into commercial use. Subsistence farmers represent an unlimited supply of labour at a wage level sufficient to satisfy the basic needs of labour in the commercial sector plus some motive for leaving peasant subsistence. The wages of labour can be viewed as their production costs, requiring given inputs of housing, food, manufactures and services. These needs may differ between farm and city jobs. With labour income corresponding to the total cost of its consumption, the value of final goods and services in the economy will equal the returns to owners of capital. If these save all their profits which become investments, the final demand in any cycle of production represents demand for investment goods. Capital produced in one period then enhances production in the following period, generating growth. In addition, with a geographical specification the need for a transport sector to ship materials and products of manufacturing and agriculture between the city and its surrounds is introduced.

Investment goods are indicated by X^I and transport services by X^T and the output of agricultural goods, manufactured consumer goods and housing by Q^1, Q^2 and Q^3. The demand for consumer goods by urban labour (L_U) and rural labour (L_R) can be represented by:

$$D_U{}^j (L_U) = Q_U{}^j \quad j = 1,2,3 \qquad\qquad 1$$

$$\text{and} \quad D_R{}^j (L_R) = Q_R{}^j \quad j = 1,2,3. \qquad\qquad 2$$

The demand for transport depends on the outputs of capital, consumer and agricultural products which necessitate shipments between town and country:

$$T (X^I, Q^1, Q^2, Q^3, Q_U^1, Q_R^2) = X^T.$$

3

The demand for consumer goods must be met from production employing capital (K) and labour (L):

$$Q_U^j + Q_R^j = Q^j = g^j (K_a^j, L_a^j) \quad j = 1,2,3.$$

4

Similarly the production of capital goods and transport employs labour and capital:

$$X^i = f^i (K_x^i, L_x^i) \quad i = I,T.$$

5

Capital stock in any period t $(K(t))$ is allocated between consumer goods and investment goods plus transport services:

$$\sum_j K_Q^j + \sum_i K_X^i \leq K (t).$$

6

For period t this total stock is that of the previous time period plus augmentation by investment over that time:

$$K (t) = K (t-1) + X^I (t-1).$$

7

The labour force of the city is given by the sum of employment in consumer goods and services, capital goods and transport service production:

$$L_U = L_{Q2} + L_{Q3} + L_X I + L_X T.$$

8

Rural employment is that in commercial agriculture:

$$L_R = L_{Q1}.$$

9

If the potential labour force $L(t)$ grows at a rate of n per period, the assumption of an unlimited supply of labour from the subsistence sector means that employment in urban and rural production will be less than the potential labour force:

$$L_U + L_R < L (t) = L (t-1) (1+n).$$

10

The equilibrium of this system is given by the configuration which maximizes the output of the investment goods industry X^I subject to the above ten relationships which constitute a soluble linear programme. If the maximum attainable rate of growth is achieved by maximizing investment, with the assumption of constant returns to scale, all other activities and employment will grow at the same rate. The rate of expansion is determined by that of capital formation, which is given by the rate of return on capital r:

$$X^I(t) = r K(t). \qquad\qquad 11$$

Thus, the rate of additions to total capital will be equal to this rate of return:

$$\frac{X^I(t)}{K(t)} = r.$$

The rate of return depends on the amount of consumption goods required to maintain labour and it must be apparent that lower sustenance costs will speed total income increase to surpass population's rise, resulting in per capita income growth. The meagre provision of housing in the Soviet Union served as well in speeding growth as Engels's inspiration in the slums of Manchester.

Geographical Policy

The chances are slim that any nation could achieve an equal velocity of growth in all its geographical parts at the same time that the national wealth is expanded most rapidly. 'Balanced' regional growth is only compatible with maximum national expansion under the unlikely circumstances that all activities are subject to constant returns to scale and all regions enjoy an equal and homogeneous share of resources. Forcing investment into inefficient locations despite price signals, for example by investment licences such as the U.K. Board of Trade Industrial Development Certificates, may produce equal growth, but only at a cost of diminished total growth. Government intervention in pricing which causes departures from marginal cost prices may lead to locational misjudgements and inefficiency. The subsidy of city passenger transport, for example, hides the true social cost of urban labour and may encourage excessive urbanization and its waste.

The existence of the agglomeration economies of Chapter 5 complicates these issues. If urbanization leads to increasing returns and decreasing costs, so total-cost-recovering prices will not give a strong enough signal to encourage desirable aggregation of activities in the central city. However, diminishing returns could be expected to bite in some activities sooner or later, pushing up urban factor prices and depressing profits. Such circumstances encourage the spill-over effects which spread investment and development into peripheral areas of low wages and land costs without government intervention.

The transport system provides channels between urban and rural markets and the optimal growth path of a realistically spacious economy must be supported by the provision of sufficient transport capacity at efficient freight rates. The recurrent theme running through our discussion of prices and trade between geographically separated markets has been of an equilibrium set of prices for a good such that inter-regional differences do not exceed the marginal cost of transport. If the freight rates charged exceed marginal transport cost, socially advantageous trade will be suppressed. Rates below marginal costs will engender trade in excess of efficient levels. Both eventualities will deter growth.

The peculiarities of the transport sector mean that it is strongly influenced in pricing and investment, if not provided, by government. Many of the difficulties which beset natural monopolies of under-investment and flexibility can be by-passed if the government provides the network and the private sector provides the vehicles and services on a competitive basis. This is the usual arrangement with road and water transport. It has not been found feasible with railways which seem to suffer from innate inflexibility and lack of response to changing demands.

Government control of transport may lead to geographical distortions caused by excessive investment in facilities. Freight rates may not reflect long-run marginal costs. This is the case with barge traffic in the U.S.A., where the Corps of Engineers provide costly dams, locks, and channels virtually without charge to the user. In such instances, the choice of manufacturing locations and agricultural products will not reflect the true cost of resources employed in transport. In the case of manufactures, such distortions are less easy to correct than most. Buildings and machinery are not readily moved and geographical momentum can soon pick up. Badly sited factories are in place for their lifetime and may attract further ill-advised investment in infrastructure and linked activities in their vicinity. The correction, of such geographical misdirection of development when detected, can be achieved by instituting proper transport pricing. It should be undertaken to prevent the compounding of geographical inefficiency generating a wasteful burden of movement and trade. Steps such as the removal of cross-subsidized branch railway services may cause considerable disruption in the short run. Such pains of transition can, however, be mitigated by temporary subsidies, to replacement road hauliers for example.

Conclusion

To conclude let us take a long and broad look at the changing geography of how man satisfies his diverse ends from scarce means. Whatever the source of the ends, the means are controlled by man's political and mechanical capabilities. These limits on control over the physical environment have been reduced through time but at an uneven pace. This we can see in the very different levels of material well-being throughout the world. The process of geographical change is visible in the spread of innovations and development through time.

A major determinant of the economic landscape as it emerges is the way in which distance is overcome to meet our needs. A society at a given state of technology will attempt to develop a transport network to minimize the total disutility of distance. Activities will competitively locate in relation to the network in such a way as to maximize the total utility of the system. Differing needs and abilities to move goods and services will result in arrays of central places and market areas, geographical specialization in production and the varying scopes of political, cultural and social territories. This differential response to the friction of distance changes over time with technical improvements in transport. Reductions in transport costs enable the drawing of larger markets and resource bases into an integrated economy. With the increase in the potential market for any good or service, the possibility exists of an increase in productivity due to the increase of trade, and specialization of production according to the comparative cost advantages of different areas. This results in the growth of service and manufacturing industries. The expansion of markets may induce the application of improved mechanical methods to production, leading to further increases in productivity and wealth. Increases in the range of markets call for geographical adjustment in the location of production to reap the most from the new set of opportunities. Activities compete for locations according to the advantages they derive from nearness to other activities, markets and resources. Broadly, those enterprises whose viability requires a greater amount of exchange with the rest of the economy will pre-empt more generally accessible locations. Service and manufacturing activities emerge as nodes of localization at strategic junctures of the network, with their geographical frequency governed by their market threshold levels. The concentration of population involved in factor-intensive activities leads to urbanization of a sector of the population.

The concentration of non-agricultural production to avoid movement costs generates further growth. Multiplicative effects of development are usually stimulated at existing towns and cities. The economies of agglomeration, which are to a major extent savings on communication and transport, and investment in urban infrastructure induce further growth at urban focuses. Traffic is heaviest and increasing most rapidly at these concentrations. Cost savings from investment will be greatest in these sections, encouraging their improvement and further increasing their attractiveness.

Further reductions in the cost of distance with investment and technical advance can again expand the scale of social and economic interaction, extending development into the periphery of the nation. The process of geographical integration involves a gradual penetration of commerce into tradition, with duality reflecting the vestiges of impermeable older ways and inhospitable terrain. The dual face of the landscape negates any simple notion of geographical equilibrium of locational patterns. However, the political attachment and intercourse of traditional with commercial regions leads to adjustment through migration, spill-over and the continual shrinkage of social and economic distance.

Appendix

The Harrod-Domar Growth Model.

(After the version of R. M. Solow, 'A contribution to growth theory',
Quarterly Journal of Economics, vol. 70, 1956, pp. 65–94.)

We trace the best path of economic expansion in terms of the relations between inputs of factors of production and output over time.

Let Y_t, K_t and L_t stand for the amounts of output, capital and labour in an economy at time t. We assume full employment of labour and capital and that there are no increasing or decreasing returns to scale. Raising all inputs n fold will raise output exactly n fold. Thus, output is a homogeneous, linear function (F) of inputs:

$$Y_t = F(K_t, L_t). \qquad 1$$

Next, it is postulated that the increase in the stock of capital occurs as a constant proportion μ of total output:

$$\frac{dK}{dt} = \mu Y. \qquad 2$$

The rate of population growth v is taken as a given exponential function of time:

$$L_t = L_o e^{vt}. \qquad 3$$

The growth path is characterized by changes over time in the ratio of capital to labour which we label:

$$Z_t = \frac{K_t}{L_t}.$$

To trace changes in Z_t we express the rate of capital accumulation in terms of this ratio and labour employed:

$$\frac{dK}{dt} = \frac{dZ}{dt}.L_t + \frac{dL}{dt}Zt$$

and since from 3, $\dfrac{dL}{dt} = vL_t$

then: $\dfrac{dK}{dt} = \dfrac{dZ}{dt}.L_t + v.Z_tL_t.$ **4**

The production relationship is now introduced to the picture and divided through by the quantity of labour to put it in per capita terms:

$F(Z_t, 1) = G(Z_t).$

Substituting back into the production function we get:

$Y_t = L_t\, G(Z_t).$ **5**

Substituting this for total output in the expression for the rate of capital accumulation yields:

$\dfrac{dK}{dt} = \mu\,(L_t)\,G(Z_t).$ **6**

If we replace the rate of change in capital in 4 with this we get the differential equation:

$\dfrac{dZ}{dt} + v\,Z_t = \mu\,G(Z_t)$

which we may divide through by Z_t to simplify into:

$\dfrac{dZ}{dt}\bigg/ Z_t = \dfrac{\mu G(Z_t) - v}{Z_t}.$ **7**

The solution to this equation gives the conditions for the existence of the equilibrium growth path. This solution is:

$Z_t = k\,e^{\int 1/2G(Z)\,dt}.\,e^{-vt}.$ **8**

Reasserting the assumption of a constant capital to labour ratio, in other words letting:

$\dfrac{dZ}{dt} = 0$

then $v.Z_t = \mu\,G(Z)$ (from 7).

Expanding the terms of this:

$v\,\dfrac{K_t}{L_t} = F\dfrac{(K_t, 1)}{L_t}$

dividing through by L_t gives:

$$= \frac{\mu}{L_t} F(K_t, L_t)$$

and from 6:

$$\frac{vK_t}{L_t} = \frac{dK}{L_t}$$

which, finally, reveals that

$$vK = dK \text{ or } v = \frac{dK}{K}. \qquad\qquad 9$$

This final statement, arising from an assumption of a constant capital-to-labour ratio, shows that the steady-state path of growth is achieved when the rate of capital accumulation (i.e. the increment to capital as a proportion of existing capital $\frac{dK}{K}$), is exactly equal to the rate at which population is expanding.

Readings

The state of the art on the mathematical theory of economic growth was summarized in 1969 by F. H. Hahn and R. C. O. Matthews, 'The theory of economic growth: a survey' in *Surveys of economic theory, Vol. II*, prepared for the Royal Economic Society and the American Economic Association, Macmillan, London, 1969, pp. 1–124.

In the same volume H. B. Chenery takes up questions of development strategy in 'Comparative advantage and development policy', op. cit., pp. 125–55.

The balanced growth view is presented by R. Nurske, *Problems of capital formation in underdeveloped countries*, Blackwell, Oxford, 1953. Intervention for unbalanced growth is advocated by A. O. Hirschman, *The strategy of economic development*, Yale University Press, New Haven, Connecticut, 1958, and G. Myrdal, *Rich lands and poor*, Harper and Row, New York, 1958.

The programming model of regional growth presented in this chapter is from L. Lefeber, 'Economic development and regional growth' in G. Fromm (ed.), *Transport investment and economic development*, Brookings Institute, Washington, D.C., 1965, pp. 108–22. This is a collection of a dozen essays directed at the transport policy issues which accompany growth management and planning.

11. Political Economy and Geography

The issues of geographical policy and regional politics, raised in the last chapter, provide the focus towards which the whole purpose of this book has been directed. The import of theory about the economy's working is that it can shed light on questions of governance. The only relevance of economics is that it informs the higher art of political economy. The point of geographical economics is to help sound judgement of the 'where?' questions of national housekeeping.

The landscape we inhabit is not an even plain whose use is determined by the instantaneous conflict of homogeneous automata. The locations of people, buildings, machinery, fields, mines, roads and transmission lines, and the volumes of things grown, made, moved and used, have been shaped by the exercise of authority as well as by lust tempered by degrees of avarice. Contests for use of land and resources have been resolved by political means. The goals of the laws and commands which have been promulgated to govern the geography of a polity are manifold and frequently at odds. The mainspring of government is the fostering of a nation's social coherence and cultural health. Good housekeeping and economic vitality are clearly a prerequisite for these. In geographical terms, this implies the sustenance of exchange and social intercourse to provide an adequate livelihood and leisure to the people of the nation. The cost of providing this must be counted not only in the land, minerals, atmosphere, waters, labour, machines and buildings used up, but also in the eddies of discontent stirred and the unrecompensed damage inflicted on others. To achieve the ends desired, control can be exerted on how land is used. Rules can be made for the places set aside for living, buying, selling and production, and the manner in which resources are acquired and goods produced. The prices of inputs and outputs or locations can be controlled through taxation. Leverage can be applied to the geographical trajectory of society by the provision of channels for trade and contact, influencing the cost of transport and communication between parts of a nation and with the rest of the world. Locations and land uses and media for transport and information have ever and everywhere been subject to legal guidance and political permission or commission.

In the last analysis these economic aspects of spatial policy concern the mechanism for allotting the national product. The problem is whether the resources to fuel the dual configurations of occupation of the land and the means of movement should be doled out on the basis of market requirements or not. If not, should some political contract, made instrumental as an administrative rubric, be employed? Failing this, should decisions be made by the case-by-case exercise of political judgement? In many instances, the economy's 'invisible hand' or cold administrative calculation may have no mandate to comprehend the complex, intangible factors involved. Only the proximate calculus and will of statesmanship, yielding a politically responsible judgement, will suffice to encompass these. This is an over-simplification of the choices confronting those who would govern; nevertheless, it will aid understanding to address issues in terms of whether they should be submitted to political authority for solution or are best left to the conciliatory mechanisms of the whole of society. One of the impressive aspects of advanced and primitive societies alike is the way in which resource allocation problems can be solved, without recourse to violence or any overriding authority, via the indiscriminate price mechanism and market transactions. The operation of markets is usually tempered by traditional and command elements, which can give rise to partiality. The type and degree of partiality which is acceptable is a matter of politics.

In general the intervention of government in the workings of the geography of the economy is best limited to three main types of action. The first is in the case of imperfect competition. A degree of monopoly can arise either from ownership of a unique resource or because an activity involves heavy initial costs and small marginal costs of production. Land exemplifies the former case and the provision of water, electricity, gas, telephones and some transport services, the latter. The second instance justifying government intervention is a misallocation of resources brought about by externalities or spill-over social costs and benefits. In the case of external costs this intervention may take the form of placing legal restrictions on the activity generating them as with land use controls. On the other hand, it may be done by internalizing the cost, such as might be achieved with a pollutant emission tax. A special case of spill-overs arises with those goods and services which are collective by nature. It would be abhorrent or impracticable to exclude people from their use on the basis of payment. The private sector could not provide these because it could not extract revenue to cover the cost of provision. Obvious examples are police, parks, libraries and roads. The third reason for intervention is for the direct redistribution of individual income if ethically unacceptable or

politically dangerous disparities threaten the social peace. Direct redistribution, through taxation, say, is certainly superior to the oft-employed
alternative of providing certain goods and services by subsidies, ostensibly
because those in authority know they are good for the poor.

Land Use, Transport and Planning

People locate their households and occupations and travel and ship their
goods because they judge that an amount of well-being to themselves will
arise which is in excess of the cost in money, effort and irritation involved
in these sites and movements. The well-being comes from the sale of their
talent, the production and vending of goods, the use of goods and amenities
and the enjoyment of life. The nearness of a place to various sources of
such benefits is mirrored in the rent paid for occupying that location. The
inherent disutility of distance in achieving the fruits of production and
consumption find expression in the combination of rent and transport
costs involved in overcoming it. In making choices of where to dwell, work,
ship, produce and disport themselves and what means of transport and
routes to associate with these activities, individuals may be misinformed
as to the real resource cost to society involved. On the supply side, owners
of land and providers of transport may not be informed by the revenue
they can achieve of effects, costly or beneficial, on their customers and
others. Those failures of the market to equate costs and utility occasion
public action. Whether the debate is over the ability of the market to do
the job, or over particular or general government decisions, the central
issue is the same: what is the best means of getting the greatest satisfaction
of the demand for space and place and their concomitant, mobility, with
the least cost to society? Questions of the desirable form of settlement
are inevitably questions about acceptable and efficient means of travel.

One means of solution is public planning. This presents the geographical
framework for the good life as an authoritative map to guide the future.
Unfortunately, for such an exercise to be effective, impossible predictions
of the future state of the world have to be made. As opposed to planning,
the market has the advantages of flexible and rapid response to changes in
taste and technology, the provision of a wide variety of options and a
continuum of provisions in answer to demands, rather than the homogeneous allotment that legislation must offer. This alternative, legislated
provision or planning implies making a decision on a common utility
for goods and services and imposing the requisite supply across the board.
Now the political calculus, which generates planning, is an intricate procedure, which moves slowly and has usually to produce uniform solutions.
If the body politic is seen to discriminate among its members, confidence

is shaken and disintegration sets in. Many goods provided publicly are so because it has been too difficult to establish and operate a market for them. The example of roads has been referred to already. If a method were devised more closely to equate use and the bearing of costs, then many of the problems of congestion and urban design associated with this collective facility would solve themselves. Nevertheless, assignment of resources by bids of buyers and sellers does sometimes fail to meet the needs of social satisfaction and requires governmental efforts. We will now consider some geographical issues where the need is disputed.

Regulation of Land Use Competition

The differentiation of geography gives every plot of land a unique value and confers the potential monopoly power arising from this on the owner. That the surplus of utility from the use of land can be captured by its owner as rent was remarked in Chapter 1. However, this results in no loss to society in efficiency terms. The equilibrium resulting from the action of a perfectly discriminating monopolist, which is what a well-articulated land market would give rise to, is identical to that resulting from perfect competition. Attempts to maximize profits when marginal revenue is equal to demand lead to prices which equal marginal costs. This is the requirement for allocative efficiency of resource use. It was also pointed out in Chapter 1, however, that welfare is a matter of equity as well as efficiency. If landowners are a small class, the concentration of income which arises may be deemed undesirable. The benefits of government-provided facilities and amenities which enhance the value of land may all accrue to landowners rather than the general population of land users, for whom they were intended. This may prompt action to collectivize the benefits of public improvements, capturing such value for more equitable redistribution. This is the intent of the community land scheme and development land tax provisions of current planning legislation in the U.K., although whether these will prove operable is as yet unclear. Ultimately, the more thoroughgoing means to the same end is the public ownership of land, and when a landed gentry and nobility to man the state is no longer called for, perhaps this is an appropriate solution. There is, however, a seeming dichotomy between bureaucracy and efficiency which puts the cost of public ownership very high.

An over-zealous attack on monopoly profits or rent emphasizes the needs of current equity to the detriment of longer term goals. Abhorrence of this surplus betrays a wholly static perspective on the economy. The prospect of gaining a profit with a new product or by penetrating a new market can be viewed as the very driving force behind the economy's expansion. In geographical terms, if the possibility of earning economic rent is removed entirely, then with it goes the private motive for seeking efficiency in the use of land. This would leave it to bureaucrats and planners to construct the social-welfare function and translate its maximization into decision rules governing land uses. Over half a century of Soviet experience suggests that this is of necessity a crude procedure. In the U.K., thirty years of strong land use control, local government ownership of much of the residential stock and government enterprise in creating new settlements have not clearly demonstrated the superiority of public planning.

The power bestowed by planning replacing competition can give rein to attempts to materialize the utopian conceits specifying the geography of the ideal *polis*, which haunt our heritage. In dreams of the New Jerusalem, the disutility of space is to be overcome by limiting the size of the settlement to avoid alienation, disintegration or whatever. This tradition, in favour of small communities and limitation, has continued, despite some notable advances in overcoming distance. This conservative inhibition, curiously mixed with whimsical, Virgilian notions concerning the joys of rural life, has resulted in the hash of anti-metropolitanism, preservationism, Green Belts, New Towns, neighbourhood units, windswept agoras and 'balanced' communities that constitute current-practice notions of Utopia. All of this has unfortunately diverted energy from the small attentions which could have made life in the existing fabric more pleasant. The slum was a cancer to be eradicated, not a wound to be healed.

Inner-city wastelands have as their root cause a decrease in employment opportunities in these areas. What functioned as vital though scruffy immigrant reception areas in Glasgow's Gorbals and New York's South Bronx, the East End of London and the South Side of Chicago, lost their momentum. Lower incomes led to failure to pay rent. Landlords cut their losses by abandonment or picking up an insurance cheque for the result of arson. Thieving, violence, dope, drunkenness and vandalism were rife. The political response was the same on both sides of the Atlantic. People were trapped where they were by the money poured into public housing and 'urban renewal' schemes. This generated its own blight as subsidized public housing speeded the rate at which private housing was abandoned and destroyed. The destruction wreaked by the public bulldozer encourages private enterprise in the same vein.

There are signs of sanity, however. In the U.K. in 1976, it was announced that the balance of industrial location policy, which had drained off jobs into new and expanded towns and development areas, would be tilted in favour of inner-city areas. This, along with housing policy encouragement for the rehabilitation rather than renewal of much of the older stock, holds some hope of stability. The Carter administration in the U.S.A. has dribbled some small amount of Federal seed-money into self-help schemes for rehabilitation.

Much of the conflict between private development and planning must be understood in terms of aesthetics. The justification for town and country planning lay partly in the firm belief that the common herd have poor taste and that competitive development, in exploiting this, will produce aesthetically immoral environments. In which sector good taste rests is hard to argue. Public and private patronage can be matched in horror and charm. Fortunately, the form of public works has often outlived the function. The cruelty and injustice their beauty served is disembodied from the monuments of tyrants and avenues for troops.

Regulating Transport Competition

The natural monopoly of all of the so-called utilities has geographical implications in terms of pricing and service provision. The sector in which intervention designed to control imperfect competition has its most profound geographical impacts is transport. The restriction and subsidy of various forms of transport structure the surface of transport costs of activities and guide locational decisions to particular outcomes in the landscape. The control of road, rail, water and air competition by manipulation of prices and entry to the field, by the provision of infrastructure or by state ownership, can determine the extent of network coverage and the geographical scope of services. In the U.S.A., the government provides a cartel for the incumbent carriers by means of the Interstate Commerce Commission and the Civil Aeronautics Board. In return it has some control on prices and assurance of stability of service. The price of this has been questioned of late and deregulation of entry and prices is well under way, in the airline industry at least. The Army Corps of Engineers gratifies an urge to build locks, dams and channels and provides barge operation with a vastly subsidized right of way. Meanwhile the Federal Highway Authority does the same for road users, but with a larger contribution from them. Recently, special agencies have been created to relieve ailing railroads of certain burdens. AMTRAK siphons off and subsidizes passenger service. The financial mess of the north-eastern railroads is to be cleaned up by the creation of a federally underwritten local monopoly, CONRAIL. In the U.K. similar cartel-like arrangements, controlling prices and entry in the interests of 'stability', resolved themselves into the monopolization and public ownership of the railways in 1948. Controls on British Rail's prices and services were gradually relaxed, so that the corporation now enjoys complete commercial freedom. After continuous draconian entry control, the road haulage industry was freed up to the discipline of the market in 1974. Apart from policing and providing roads, the government's major contribution is to cover the ever-mounting losses of British Rail.

The effective policy question which dominates in all countries where different modes compete for traffic is that of subsidy. Whether it be in the form of providing facilities at less than cost or covering financial losses, government's effect on the extent of service networks and the transport cost structure of the nation works through the disbursement of subsidies.

The general case for subsidizing provision of a good is that its production is subject to decreasing costs. In order to ensure the efficient allocation of resources between different uses, the cost and revenue from the last unit of output sold should be equal. If costs are a decreasing function of output, to charge a price that satisfied this requirement would produce insufficient revenue to cover total costs. Total cost is given by average cost of production times the number of units of output. It is obvious that if costs are decreasing as output expands, then the cost of the last unit produced is always less than the average cost of all the previous units produced. It has been argued that a subsidy is necessary in such circumstances to cover the gap between efficient prices, registering the utility of the good for the rest of the economy to note, and the costs of the producer. There is a body of opinion which holds that railways enjoy decreasing costs and, thus, warrant subsidy.

It is not clear that beneath the complexity of rail-cost relations there is a decline of cost with output. In the U.S.A. evidence suggests that costs increase proportionally with increases in traffic and that the dense north-eastern railroads, closest in character to the British network, exhibit no economies of scale. It has been suggested, in vitiation of the subsidy argument, that British Rail costs can be reduced with decreasing output by tailoring track and signalling expenditures to the volume of traffic to avoid surplus capacity. The traditional way of covering the gap between the sum of average costs and total revenue has been to discriminate in prices between customers according to how badly they need to use a service, i.e. their elasticity of demand. The Interstate Commerce Commission's brief excludes this course of action in the U.S.A. British Rail has the remit to do this but has shown a reluctance, which must stem from the lack of commercial motive of management.

In the case of rail inter-city passenger services, it seems reasonable to postulate that they could be made to pay financially by a combination of price rises and cost cuts, even if at the expense of thinning out the frequency and coverage of services. AMTRAK in the U.S.A. was intended to be commercially viable, but its extent is subject to pork-barrel politics and its clientele is old, poor and few, so that a subsidy for national pride of a passenger rail system may mount. In the U.K., covering the current deficit of passenger services out of the Exchequer is almost certainly shifting income towards the better off. There seems no obvious reason why bigger, less frequent trains, with the same reliability, should not maintain custom and improve load factors, given that rail travel is not an impulse purchase but planned. In rural areas of the U.K. it seems so clear that a generous level of road service to those captive to public transport, in terms of defraying either taxi or bus expenses, could be provided at vastly less than stopping train services, as to brook no argument.

Governments do provide facilities for some forms of transport so that they are not required to pay for the resources used in their tracks or way fully. We have seen that in the U.S.A. the ardour of the Corps of Engineers to pour concrete and dredge mud is not requited by payments from water carriers. Evidence suggests that road freight operators in both the U.K. and U.S.A. are subsidized in their use of roads. The argument is made that the competitive imbalance created by their circumstances should be corrected by awarding rail operators a compensating subsidy. The more straightforward increases of charges to water and road carriers would seem a more efficacious way of improving welfare. One major characteristic of freight transport which militates against such subsidy proposals is the evident unresponsiveness of demand to the stimulus of price changes. Demand for freight movement is more strongly determined by geographical and qualitative considerations than by price. There is no single, ideal form of freight shipment and a variety of facilities have to be used to meet different time, place and quality specific requirements. The adjustment process to changes in the price of transport relative to other inputs is a locational one, with an accordingly long time period for its completion. Some changes of transport mode require capital investment in loading and unloading facilities and batch-size-related equipment on the part of the customer, which is another inhibition to price responsiveness. Given that the demand for movement of freight by a particular mode shows little sensitivity to changes in its own price or that of competing modes, a subsidy to rail freight services will give little rise to improvement in the performance of the economy as a whole, and will merely transfer funds from taxpayers to existing rail freight users.

Externalities

A further general reason for dissatisfaction with the ability of an unbridled market solution to determine where to locate things and how and where to move people and goods can be summarized in the term 'externalities'. These are costs and benefits which spill over from an activity to impinge on others. The perpetrators see no reflection of these impacts in the prices facing them and, therefore, are not swayed by such externalities in making consumption or production decisions. Obnoxious land uses, generating smoke, smell and noise, are a case in point. Land-use planning controls and zoning laws in the U.S.A. were enacted to keep incompatible uses of land separate. This segregative power of local governments is a rich source of corruption and has probably done general harm in separating work and home places unnecessarily in the urban texture at a time when the noisome nature of factories has subsided with new technology. Transport use of land is clearly one of the chief sources of gas, particles, noise and danger and has more widespread effects than most.

The treatment of these matters by government comes down to the evaluation of the worth of public works or private investments upon which public leverage can be exerted. Government can insist on accounting the merits of alternative courses of action inclusive of the indirect impacts on the well-being of all members of society. In response to an increase in popular sensitivity to nuisance and danger, efforts are being made to incorporate the external effects on non-participants in the decision process. Environmental impact statements are required for major projects involving federal funds in the U.S.A. Citizen pressure groups, seeking the sanction of the law against degradation of the environment, have provided for elaborate public review through litigation.

The physical measurement of noise, air pollutants and visual intrusion and prediction of levels of these associated with specific traffic volumes on roads of different configurations, for example, is fairly well developed. However, even the physical magnitude of some potential impacts is in contention. The dangers associated with atomic power plants are in dispute, in public debate at least. Where physical outcomes are predictable, it is possible to judge between alternative ways of meeting the same need. For example, a sunken or elevated profile for a piece of road or several locations for an airport can be compared in terms of the numbers of people disturbed by the undesirable levels of intrusive effects. The residents within a certain noise-contour line can be counted. Any difference in costs between options can be judged against the external effects one at a time. An explicit value judgement can be made of the relative importance of different effects and their values can be turned into standardized scores, weighted and aggregated to produce a composite disamenity score for each option. Only a politician has the credentials to specify the weights and impose decisions made on this basis on society. Being highly sensitive to the fickleness of taste, politicians are notoriously and, perhaps, rightly shy of allowing their judgement to be quantified in such a fashion. Even if such an exercise were feasible, it falls short with decisions on different projects in different places, e.g. a coal-power plant versus a hydro-electric scheme. In such cases values in common units, i.e. in terms of money, have to be applied to measures of intrusion and nuisance, the benefits to users and the costs involved, if a comparable trade-off or rate of return is to be estimated. Money values must be assessed for external impacts if a consistent convention is to decide such matters. One possible recourse is to look at the preferences which people reveal in the market. An attempt can be made to isolate the differences in house prices which can be attributed solely to their degree of exposure to noise. The complexity of the housing market and the package of qualities purchased with a residence make it well nigh impossible to separate out one attribute of desirability. Observations of house price differences often suggest private reactions to noise quite at odds with public pronouncements on the value of quiet. Results of asking people how important peace and quiet are to them are of little use. Those in quiet locales proclaim its supremacy while those beside sources of unquiet register indifference. The gap between perception and substance presents additional confusion. The main pollutant from motor vehicles which has a deleterious effect on health is carbon monoxide, which is imperceptible. Diesel fumes and smoke from lorries, which are the main occasion of public outcry, are relatively innocuous. It does seem that the difficulties of arriving at sensible and generally acceptable prices for peace, quiet and clean air will preclude their mechanical inclusion in cost and benefit calculations. There is, however, one instance in which the public sector has acknowledged a debt and made a regular arrangement for compensation. The U.K. Land Compensation Act 1973 requires the payment of compensation for adverse environmental effects, especially noise, caused by new road schemes. This is not, however, retroactive. In general, given the difficulty of evaluating the physical measures of spill-overs, the conflicts arising will mostly be answered by legislation of minimum acceptable standards with violation subject to prosecution. The Clean Air Act proved a successful exercise of this nature in the U.K. The Environmental Protection Agency's automobile emission standards, binding on manufacturers, are struggling into existence in the U.S.A.

The existence of negative externalities has been used in arguments for subsidies for forms of production which generate less clamour, stench and loss of life and limb. Pro-rail interests have mounted this campaign directed against road freight operations. The fact is that the railway network does not have the capacity to reduce significantly the volume of road traffic in the right places. In addition, responsiveness to changes in each other's prices between modes is such that a subsidy would result in little change. The environmentally damaging impact of road vehicles is most felt in built-up areas and, given that many rail services require local road delivery, then transfer to rail would tend to concentrate the nuisance of moving goods from the edges of town to the centres. Similar lines of argument have been deployed to justify commuter rail facilities. It is proposed that by attracting people to rail travel, car mileage and its effects will be reduced. Actual cases do not inevitably support this contention. In California, the Bay Area Rapid Transit system's inception led to an increase in car travel per head. People who formerly walked to the corner to get a bus into San Francisco began to drive to the infrequently distributed railway stations. The main target of opinion in favour of public transport subsidy to reduce externalities is road congestion. This phenomenon was examined in Chapter 6. There is a widely-held notion that a subsidy to public transport, compensation for the misconceived and collective costs of road congestion, will produce a significant reduction in road traffic. This seems unlikely. The major determinant of car use is car availability. Use does not vary much in response to cost differentials between modes of transport. The advantages of the car for more diffuse geographical circumstances seem so far in excess of anything that public transport can offer, that even free service will not bring about a return to the bus and train. Price reductions and service improvements mostly attract people who would otherwise have stayed put or walked. The most important factor in a driver's perception of the relative advantage of the car over other means of travel is the availability and price of parking. Parking charges which reflect the opportunity cost of the land used and any structures involved would in most towns bring a level of demand and road network performance not far removed from the socially desired optimum. Regarding the restraint and pricing policies discussed in Chapter 3, it is evident that even major cities have achieved congestion equilibria at tolerable speed levels, without utter chaos or seizure. In judging the efficiency of the present situation against the possible results of more stringent restraint, such as road pricing or supplementary licensing, distributional implications must be considered. It can be argued that rationing of a fixed supply by a queue, which is what congestion does, results in a progressive redistribution of income. Price rationing is regressive. The poorer value time less highly in terms of money than the rich. An additional effect of this is that time penalties, rather than prices, may be more effective in reducing the peak of congestion by spreading out the time at which people travel. Time penalties bite on those with higher values of time. Lower income people, with lower values of time, are mostly governed by fixed work hours. On the other hand, higher income, managerial and supervisory workers, whose time values are usually higher, often have a greater degree of discretion as to when their work day starts and ends.

Redistributive Goals

The need or desire to temper efficiency with equity gives us the third ground for policing the economy. A more equable sharing of the nation's wealth is best accomplished directly, by taxes and transfer payments. However, government control over the provision of certain goods and services and over the location of infrastructure and land uses has been used with redistributive intent. The supply of many collective goods is regulated with the intention of influencing incomes. Other goods, though not essentially collective, are treated as special and subsidized for some or all of the population. Education, health services and housing are cases in point. In practice the effect can sometimes go contrary to the intention. This is especially true in the U.K.'s partly public housing arrangements. The vagaries of waiting lists and tests of worthiness often put comparatively well-off older people with grown-up children in subsidized housing. The needier and younger with small children and new arrivals are thrown upon a truncated rental market, constrained in supply by price control and a lack of security of disposal for landlords. The rentals charged for local-authority housing bear little relation to costs of provision or rents in the private sector. They certainly do not reflect the comparative advantage of locations, thus throwing one of the welfare equilibriating mechanisms of the market into confusion.

The Regional Distribution of Wealth

The main explicitly geographical intervention in pursuit of greater equity is to be found where policy instruments are brought to bear on the distribution of activities and income between parts of the nation. These seek to redress persistent unemployment in some areas due to structural changes in the economy. This is to be found on the coalfields of Highland Britain's carboniferous edge, in the shipyards of the Tyne, Clyde and Belfast Lough, in the cotton mill towns in New England, the Nord and Lancashire and in the mechanized rural South. High levels of unemployment imply low incomes. Low incomes can also arise from underemployment, such as might be found in the traditionally organized, rural section of a nation – in Appalachia, the Atlantic fringe of the British Isles, in Italy's Mezzogiorno and, indeed, in most of the world. In many countries 'regional' policies providing special subsidies for firms which locate in such depressed areas are offered by central or local government. In the U.K. the stick and carrot sanction of Industrial Development Certificates has been used to steer industrialists in locating factories. This is reinforced by relief from payroll tax and the favoured treatment of designated areas as far as infrastructure and social service expenditure grants from central government are concerned.

There seems no doubt that the Local Employment Act of 1963 and subsequent inducements have brought about a shift of jobs to designated target areas in the U.K. It has been calculated that by 1970 this amounted to some 15,000 jobs a year. This certainly increased employment and incomes in these regions and reduced migration from them (except from Scotland). Whether the policies reduced the differences in unemployment and income between regions significantly is doubtful. The most that can be said on the evidence is that the gaps between the more prosperous and depressed regions were not allowed to widen. The opportunity cost of this was the loss of jobs for the growth regions of the economy – London and the West Midlands. These are by no means areas of uniform prosperity and overheated labour markets. The draining-off of employment may well have exacerbated the inner-city decay problems of London in particular and generated some of the external costs that accompany unemployment. It was in recognition of this that Peter Shore made the pronouncement on location policy in 1976 referred to when we discussed the treatment of urban blight.

In the treatment of growth in Chapter 10, it was pointed out that equi-proportional growth among all regions of an economy was likely only under the most unusual circumstances. The redistribution of existing output or of the increment of output to achieve equality of mean income between parts of a country can only be bought by a reduction in efficiency and the rate of growth. The determination of the right balance of efficiency and equity in this case, as with every other we have considered here, is a matter for statecraft. Economics can analyse such quandaries and inform judgements but cannot pretend to know facts about the ways of the world which will yield an objective solution to the problem.

One unscientific and rhetorical sin which confuses debate over geo-graphical resource allocation policy is the personification of territory embodied in the 'regional' tag. Few would openly oppose the proposition that the highest good is individual freedom of choice, which should only be curbed if its exercise harms others. This underlying axiom of our culture has been confused by reference to 'regional' well-being, balance and prosperity. Regions become more than mere territory but organic wholes, greater than the sum of their inhabitants, with ends of their own. Such sophistry is a demagogic trick. It is designed to create a sense of identity which will emotionally overwhelm self-interest with a figment. This resort is employed to shore up political power bases eroded by changing economic circumstances. In the U.K. intervention in the pattern of industrial development and population change was advocated on the grounds that decreases in population caused harm to 'the community life in denuded areas'. Such a proclamation attempts to imbue locality with similar magic to working-class solidarity. It offers shelter from the bewilderment of the social agoraphobia which new-found freedom and wider horizons may cause. Promoters of regional identity presume that no right-minded person would wish to leave his native soil. The policy implication of this view is that everyone should be enabled to stay where they were born. This lack of geographical venturesomeness, expressing fear of change, is hardly in keeping with Marxist dialectic as a guide to life. Its attitude to place is feudal, if not tribal. Combined with this is an uncritical acceptance of the competitive processes which brought the present distribution about. In the U.K. this belief in the market appears to have an historical discontinuity about 1930, when the imperial, coalfield economy began to crumble.

One objective which is put forward for regional policy is that each region should receive its 'proper' share of economic expansion. Historically it is clear that such a directive in the last century would have stunted the take-off into sustained growth of Britain, Western Europe and the U.S.A. It can be countered that many growing industries today are 'footloose', making a more even spread of growth viable. Experience, however, has shown that there are variations in locational advantage and that the degree of indifference between regions of industries has been seriously over-estimated, even beyond the range of the financial inducements offered for locating in depressed areas. There are, nevertheless, voices for more extreme measures. Some insist that productive capacity should be redistributed so as to achieve regional income equality, even at the expense of the growth of the national economy. The argument in favour of maximizing growth in order to increase the general living standard, rather than redistribution among income groups, certainly holds true for redistribution among regions of a country. The general living standard is raised more rapidly by maximizing the rate of growth rather than by redistributing income. A politically feasible readjustment, which would halt total growth, might give a once-and-for-all rise of incomes in depressed areas by 10 per cent. This could be accomplished, without reducing anyone's income, by a national growth rate of 3 per cent per annum in about three years.

A recent source of inspiration for the regional protectionist case is in the Galbraithian 'quality of life' crusade. This attitude would gladly sacrifice growth to redress the balance of 'private affluence versus public squalor'. Its drawback is that it shows little feeling for the aspirations of the vast mass of people. To be willing to forgo private affluence on other people's behalf, before they have ever tasted comfort and can decide for themselves, shows a fine aristocratic contempt. From a global perspective, for the developed world to put the brake on its rate of growth bodes ill for the hopes of the poverty-stricken. In a world where the separating power of distance is diminished daily, our notions of welfare and society owe more than lip-service to cosmopolitan responsibilities.

Readings

The texts by Hoover, Richardson and Nourse, cited at the end of Chapter 9, all have policy as their focus. Combined with R. L. Bish and H. O. Nourse, *Urban economics and policy analysis*, McGraw-Hill, New York, 1975, they provide a thorough coverage of geographical political economy in the U.S.A.

The state of geographical affairs in the U.K., as the polity attempts to reconcile equity with efficiency, is the subject of a collection of essays edited by R. Davies and P. Hall, *Issues in urban society*, Penguin Books, London, 1978.

Index